TABLE OF CONTENTS

ACKNOWLEDGEMENTS 3
PROGRAM 7
INTRODUCTION 9
6th Grade 13
    Mithran Karthic 14
    Lawrence Liao 18
    Florence Ou 20
    Khanh Pham 31
    Ella Zimmerman 34
    Kristian Carpenter 38
    Reya Ganesh 41
    Madeleine Lee 45
    Aria Roy 47
    Dilshan Prakash 50
7th Grade 57
    Juno Seigel 58
    Jitu Abebe 61
    Sofia Ou 66
    Sufyana Johnson 74
    Asha Smith 77
    Arya Das 79
    Melanie Ouyang 81
8th Grade 103
    Hridaan Popuri 104
    Lila Briskin-Watson 109

Jenny Ryu	111
Lucie Vidh	115
Luna Hernandez	120
Sophie Levine	121
INDEX	**127**

ACKNOWLEDGEMENTS

Celebrating Diversity through Creative Writing is a collaborative partnership between Friends of the Library, Montgomery County (FOLMC); Montgomery County Public Schools (MCPS); and Montgomery County Public Libraries (MCPL). As proponents of books, reading, writing, and learning, the partners of this project continue to work to evolve the program to support the talent and growth of the young people in our community.

To everyone who worked to make this year successful, especially the teachers and parents who support the students and encourage their growth and success each day, thank you. An additional thank you to our MCPS Coordinator, Secondary ELA & Literacy Specialist Miriam Plotinsky.

For the 2023-2024 school year, we were able to award students with Student Service Learning hours for participating in the program, engaging with other students, and helping each other work on Mosaic entries.

Thank you to the judges for volunteering their time and lending their expertise to the project:

- Dr. Sherri Bale, Community Member
- Larissa Johnson, FOLMC, Trustee
- Paige Kisner, Community Member
- Frances Pipa, MCPS, Student
- Lavertes Ragland, MCPL
- Charlene Saportin Disler, Community Member

- Susan Stimak, Community Member
- Abigail Wu, MCPS, Student

Thank you to Shelley Johnson Carey and Margo Brenner Collins (FOLMC, Trustees) for assisting in the editing of this anthology.

And, most importantly, congratulations to our students, who were creative and honest in their writing.

Cover Art by
Maraki Zenebe
Grade 7, Cabin John Middle School

Friends of the Library, Montgomery County (FOLMC) is a 501(c)(3) nonprofit that provides supplemental funding, programs, and materials and equipment to MCPL to augment public funding. As an independent nonprofit, FOLMC has operated for over 40 years without relying on government funding; it is not part of Montgomery County Government or MCPL.

Our mission is to strengthen, promote, and champion Montgomery County Public Libraries (MCPL), for it to better serve the learning interests and needs of the diverse and changing communities of the County.

For more information, please visit https://www.folmc.org/.

MCPL provides equitable access to information, ideas, and experiences that spark imagination and expand possibilities for all.

To explore the collections, please visit https://montgomerycountymd.gov/library/index.html.

PROGRAM

Shortly after joining FOLMC, Executive Director Ari Brooks began working with education advocates Siham Eldadah and Irene Coleman on a creative writing project modeled on their successful *Understanding Diversity through Art* program. They reached out to MCPS and began working with Latrice Rogers of the Department of Curriculum and Instruction to develop the program. After a year of planning, the first invitation for the *Celebrating Diversity through Creative Writing* contest was sent to all 38 Montgomery County Middle Schools.

Through this program, teachers at participating middle schools incorporate the theme of diversity into their lesson plans and invite students to submit an essay, poem, or short story, creatively expressing their personal reflections on diversity and/or their culture.

From each school, a teacher facilitates the selection of the top five works from each grade level to represent the school in the writing contest. The selected entries are then forwarded to the contest judges who score each entry based on the following criteria, designed to reward cultural expression, creativity, and technical skills:

Essay Expresses thoughts in a clear, focused, and insightful way. Shares relevant cultural examples and details to effectively support the theme. Includes precise word choice and evocative language.

Poem Organizes the poem in a clear manner. Employs poetic devices creatively to highlight her or his culture. Includes precise word choice and evocative language.

Short Story Develops the story skillfully, creating a vivid impression. Uses narrative devices to convey a theme of cultural diversity. Includes precise word choice and evocative language.

Judges award points for each category for a total possible score of 45 points. Each judge is encouraged to write comments that are used to determine a winner in the case of a tie. FOLMC staff then collects and tallies the scores and notifies the winners and honorable mentions for each category and grade level.

Each year, the entries of the winners and honorable mentions are collected and published in celebration of the program. The published works in this book have been edited for basic technical errors, such as spelling, but each student's submission style and body remains unchanged.

FOLMC and our partners are proud to present this inspiring collection of works from the middle school students of MCPS. The *Celebrating Diversity through Creative Writing* program has successfully enabled the opportunity for young writers to share their cultures. Their talent and passion are evident in their writing, and we hope that you enjoy their book.

INTRODUCTION

I am thrilled to write the forward for the 2024 Mosaic Anthology. What a treat!

I would've loved an opportunity like this when I was younger. To share my thoughts, curiosities, apprehensions and hopes. And maybe, just maybe, a fear or two well-disguised in the life of my characters.

The chance to share my stories.

I come from a family of storytellers and travelers (and yes, to me, they often go hand-in-hand). And when I was young, I used to search out (and devour) stories in each and every place we visited. Countless tales of people standing up and speaking out. Of people protecting and nurturing what and who they loved. Stories about family, adventure, commitment and love. Stories that showcased people's voices, their hopes, fears and dreams. Stories I could see myself in. Stories that let me know more about the world. But most importantly, stories that encouraged me to be a better, braver, more present version of myself.

No matter where we traveled in the states or abroad, I asked a million and one questions after hearing these stories, and often got the same reply from my parents. "Go look it up." But unfortunately, many of the places we visited and the stories and people we learned about were not featured in the books I read or found. They were histories and experiences that often went overlooked and ignored by the wider world.

Stories deemed unworthy of telling and knowing. But thankfully, not everyone agreed with this belief, and many of these histories and stories were passed down within communities, families and through the most curious and intrepid souls. They were the stories that I wanted to know. The stories I wanted to read. The stories I wanted to write. Stories about people that often looked like me and members of my family. Stories of bravery, determination, and sacrifice. Stories of joy, community, laughter and love. Stories that made me want to stand a little taller (Yep, stories do have the power to do that. Not only for those who read them, but for those who write them and share them as well).

Stories are that magical!

Once we would get home from a trip, my questions often multiplied "Why did that happen?" "What did they do before that?" "What did they do after?" My frustrations grew with no sources for answers and my curiosities never truly quieted until one day my parents asked, "What do you think happened?"

That simple question freed me to explore all that whirled in my mind about the lives and communities we visited and learned about. Soon, some of those people and places inspired many of my first characters, settings and stories. A mash-up of fact and fiction. A weaving together of real and imagined. Worlds filled with my imaginings and glimpses of the real-life moments I learned about and hoped to share with others. I am forever grateful to my parents for asking that simple, yet powerful question and for sharing a small part of the world with me.

Back then, I didn't realize the enormous amount of courage it also takes to put words on paper with the intention of sharing them with the world. But it does.

Each story in this anthology is an act of bravery, commitment and love, just like those stories I learned on my travels. And each writer in this anthology has the power to be a truthteller. I am honored to help in some small way to welcome these stories and their creators into the world.

Happy reading, everyone!

Leah Henderson
Author
www.leahhendersonbooks.com

6th Grade
Winners & Honorable Mentions

Untitled

Mithran Karthic

Julius West Middle School

I speak the language Tamil and did you know that it is the oldest language still spoken today? Tamil has been around for about 5,000 years!!! In all that time, you'd expect the language to be extinct, but it has survived through rich literature and connections all throughout the world. One of the celebrations that bring us all together is Pongal. Pongal lasts four days and for all four days we celebrate something different.

The first day of Pongal is Bhogi Pongal. On this day, you tidy up the house, buy new clothes, re-paint your house, rearrange, and get ready for the auspicious days ahead of you. On this day, you can dedicate the whole day to thoroughly re-arrange and clean up the house. "Pazhayana Kazhithal ; Puthiyana Puhuthal" is a phrase in Tamil. It means get rid of the old things, and buy new ones to use. This is a phrase especially used on Bhogi Pongal because it fits right in. You just find what is bad/old and get it out and get something new. This is something I enjoy because I get new things too.

The second day is where Pongal gets its name from, so it's the most important day of the tradition. The second day's name is Kathirava Pongal. Kathiravan means Sun. On this day, we wake up early in the morning and make colorful Kolam, which is also known as Rangoli. After that, we do the most important tradition of all. Everyone gets together and celebrates Pongal with a feast. Before that we pour milk into a clay pot and start to heat it up. Soon the milk will start to overflow and flood over the top. When this happens, everyone shouts "Pongalo Pongal" many times. After a while, people go to cook some tasty dishes such as pongal. There are actually two dishes called pongal. One is the sweet type of pongal, and another one is venpongal, which is made with black peppers in it, that can have different gravies on it. Both of these dishes are actually mainly made from rice. Rice is usually the main structure. You can also find sugar cane and palm jaggery in the sweet pongal, but not in venpongal. In venpongal, it is best if you put a lot of ghee which is clarified butter. Once the cooking is done, everyone gets together and shares sweet and tasty dishes.

The third day is my favorite, Maatu Pongal. Maadu means cow/bull. This is where we celebrate, respect and show our love to the cows that help farmers who give us our food. This is also when my favorite tradition happens: Jallikattu! Jallikattu has been a tradition for thousands of years. Jallikattu is when a group of brave men try to hold a bull's hump for a certain distance. Each bull is released one at a time. Only one man can hold a bull's hump at once. If someone is able to do this, they get a prize, but if the bull is able to fend off these brave men, the bull wins and the bull and its owner get a prize. Jallikattu is most famous in a city called Madurai that is in Tamil Nadu. The best Jallikattu usually happens at Alanganallur, Madurai.

The fourth day of Pongal is Kaanum Pongal. We visit our relatives on this day. This is the day we celebrate Tamil poet Thirvalluvar, so this day is also known as Thiruvalluvar day. Thiruvalluvar has given down his teachings through Thirukural. Thirukural taught me respect, kindness, and all the loyalty traits. Thirukural has been translated to many languages such as English, German, French, etc. Because of his teachings, I am the person I am today.

As I have said before my mother tongue is Tamil, and it originates from Tamil Nadu. Tamil is the language and Nadu means country, so overall, I come from Tamil country, as in TamilNadu.

We have many different games, such as Kabaddi. In Kabaddi, there are 2 teams of five. The first team that goes on offense must send in one player that must keep saying "Kabaddi" without breathing once he crosses the white line as he travels into the opponent's side.

He may tag as many players as he wants, but once he does that he must reach the white line in the middle. The defending team must try and catch the person and stop the person from touching the white line.

If the offensive player tags someone and touches the white line, the man he tagged is out, but if the defending team, all five people, trap him and keep from touching the white line, the offensive man is out.

After this happens both teams switch. If the new attacking team tags a player and gets him out, he may choose a teammate to bring back in. This process will continue until there is no one left on one team. Of course, there are more games and activities such as 'Silambaatam' and Sottangal, but if I tried naming them all, it would take too long.

At the end of these four days of Pongal you just have a feeling that fills the heart. On each of these days you feel something special and you love it! When everything is over, the energy is still there. You get to see family and friends, and eat very, very tasty food. You get to watch fun sports and can often participate! I hope someday, everyone will recognize this festival and celebrate it together.

This is my culture and I am happy to share it with you.

Chinese Culture
Lawrence Liao

Best in Show
Eastern Middle School

In a land of ancient mystery and grace,
Lies a culture so vibrant, so hard to embrace,
Chinese traditions painted with colors so bright,
Unveiling stories that echo through the night.

Silk whispers of emperors and their reigns,
Dynasties of power, a kingdom not in vain,
Dragon dances ignite the hearts of the crowd,
Symbolizing luck and blessings endowed.

The Great Wall stands tall, a testament of might,
Guarding the nation, a beacon in the night,
With every brick and stone, a tale untold,
Of unity and strength, a history so bold.

Calligraphy strokes dance upon a blank page,
A symphony of characters, wisdom to engage,
Poems and prose, cherished and revered,
Capturing emotions, love, or fear.

Tea ceremonies, a sacred art of tranquility,
Brewing leaves, a symbol of serenity,
Drinking in stories passed down through time,
Savoring the flavors, strange yet sublime.

Ancient festivals bring the streets alive,
Lanterns aglow, lighting up the sky,
Mid-Autumn's mooncakes, sweet delights,
Family reunions under dazzling lantern lights.

The gentle melodies of traditional tunes,
Erhu and Guzheng, played under moons,
Resonating through hearts, a harmonious blend,
Mesmerizing spirits, to this culture we commend.

Chinese culture, a treasure trove untold,
With customs and traditions, precious like gold,
For in this captivating tapestry of grace,
Lies a heritage that time will never erase.

A Special Dragon Painting
Florence Ou
Eastern Middle School

The wind chimes created a melodious song as the songbirds sang their throaty calls. Flapping their wings, herons slowly waded through the shallow pond as the koi gaped dumbly at the birds, aghast at their size and power. Buzzing softly, lofty dragonflies flew here and there, observing the peaceful scene of Guangzhou as they occasionally landed on the jade-green lily pads nearby. The flaps of wings, the buzzing of bugs, and the ripples of the pond joined into the birds' heavenly song. The town that rested beside the lively pond was, in contrast, silent, and resisted the young busy splendor of the pond. Cobwebs filled every crack and nook of the little buildings, and the bricks were far from their prime, being beaten and worn by time. But their color and shine could not be ignored. On the rooftops bore paintings of dragons and creatures of legend, while the door gods, MenShen, were sculpted and glossed with magnificent shades of red. However, the soft rain rode off almost all the visitors — ("I prefer to visit on sunny days," one huffed snootily) — in such a way that the cobblestone streets deserted.

The workers who managed the place simply returned home, knowing there was no point in waiting for tourists. Who would come here in the rain? Nobody liked being wet, cold, and soggy while trying to appreciate the buildings from thousands of years ago. So they left the village to itself and drove back to their warm, comfy houses, where they enjoyed doing who-knows-what.

As the last of them departed, the gong on the hill nearby rang loudly into the quiet atmosphere, signaling that the area was closed. No more visitors allowed…

…Except for the janitor, of course. He was tasked with cleaning the central building, a large, proud temple that sat alongside the gong. Despite the temple's grand and clean demeanor, the manager required that every inch was scrubbed into perfection at the end of the day to preserve its "cleanliness." Unfortunately, ZhenZhu, the janitor, was infamous among the workers for hating his job. He was known to be especially grumpy when cleaning the temple and always wore a trademark scowl (not that the manager minded, of course). You could imagine his face when he marched into the building, dirty mop in hand and dragging behind a muddy pail of water. "Fiddlesticks," he mumbled, glaring at the vast room. Lo and behold! On the walls held rows and rows of parchment, each splashed with arrangements of ink and paint, morphing into forms of beautiful ladies clothed in dresses, immortals riding on clouds, and tigers colored red, orange, and radiant black. Each painting had Chinese letters scrawled on the paper in a messy yet artistic fashion, telling tales of old.

All ZhenZhu wanted to do was clean the whole place and get done with it. He didn't care about art and never had a taste for it. What was the point of ink and paint, really? Shuffling side to side, the grumpy janitor hastily mopped his way forward, using his duster to clean the walls as he stomped past columns. After 20 boring (yet rather quick) minutes, he finally reached the last painting at the end of the corridor. Hanging between two golden pillars, it was the largest by far, depicting a dragon flying through the clouds as it entangled itself into a network of scales. In its vast talons was a flaming pearl the size of a round gold nugget.

Though he never admitted it, ZhenZhu's only exception for his hatred towards art was this one. It was big! Lovely! Exceptional! Sometimes, he would even stand in front of the dragon, staring wide-eyed at the details in awe…but soon enough, he would recover from his trance, snort, and leave the temple.

This time, however, there was something different about the painting. Now, standing in front of the dragon as he had done many times before, there was a somewhat connection. Heart fluttering like a Red-whiskered Bulbul, ZhenZhu felt himself pulling towards the parchment as if a magical force was urging him to come closer….

Closer…and closer, until he was face-to-face with the dragon….suddenly, real, scaly talons emerged from the parchment and pulled him through.

"ARGHHHHHHHHHHHHHHHHH!" the janitor screeched as the floor seemed to disappear from under him. The gold walls of the temple evaporated and he found himself plunging through a crystal blue sky, falling through puffy clouds and plummeting towards death. Screaming frantically, he closed his eyes, flailed his arms, and prepared for his sudden last breaths until two sets of sharp claws caught him from above. "Relax," rumbled a strong, mighty voice. ZhenZhu, thankful that he was still alive, peered at the source, squinting at the heavenly figure haloed behind the sunlight like an angel….until he realized that this so-called angel had long, massive talons the size of swords, a hulking, snaky body covered with scales, and a snout, lined with whiskers and surrounded by a long, lion-like mane. Grabbing his shoulders with two rough palms and looking at him with black beetle eyes was—could it be?—a dragon. It was the exact replica of the one in the painting just minutes ago.

ZhenZhu screamed again, writhing in the dragon's grip and blubbering all sorts of nonsense. It seemed like he wasn't ready to relax just yet. Sighing, the dragon said, "I suppose it's normal for humans to panic whenever this happens. But let me start with a formal introduction, shall I? I am Honglong the red dragon, at your service. And you are?" Zhenzhu, whose sanity seemed to have disappeared completely, whimpered: "Mishmashgobbleplopblubber…" "Ah well, my dear Mishmash!" cried the dragon, beaming and oblivious to ZhenZhu's crazed answer. "I'll just call you that for short."

"Zhen….zhu…." came the feeble reply. "My….name….is ZhenZhu…." Then the poor janitor went back to blubbering nonsense. A pause. "Ah, why didn't you say that earlier?" asked Honglong, trying to ignore the enormous word vomit. Placing ZhenZhu on his back, the eastern dragon explained, "Though that wasn't the greatest introduction, ZhenZhu, I'm pleased to meet you. Every century I can connect with the literal world to help a fellow human! Whether it's an emperor, a peasant, whatever! I am very old, despite my young appearance, so it is natural for me to assist young ones in need."

"You...you pulled me through a piece of parchment!" said ZhenZhu, aghast. "Precisely. I opened a portal into literature, arts, and music! Where everything invented by the creativity of the human mind comes to life! Like me, for example," replied Honglong. ZhenZhu paled in surprise. "All I see are some clouds."

"Which is why you must hold on tight!"

"What the—"

Like an arrow, the dragon expertly plunged downwards, shooting toward the ground like a crazy missile. ZhenZhu felt the wind brutally slap his 57-year-old face like an old rock on the pavement being kicked by a child. Lost for words and unable to scream at such speed, ZhenZhu followed Honglong's advice and held on to his elegant copper mane. In about 30 seconds they reached the earthy ground, where willows flourished near shimmering rivers and deer pranced around in the grass. Hovering just above some oaks nearby, Honglong said, "This [is] the territory where your culture thrives!" Brandishing his talons towards the sky, the janitor squinted up (ZhenZhu was in terrible need of glasses) to see other dragons of different colors and sizes, some round and good-mannered, other slim with glitters splattered on their scales, others mixtures of both, and more. ZhenZhu, though flabbergasted to see living mythical creatures, growled, "I see no importance in culture."

"Which is why you need help, young one!" replied Honglong. "Culture is a part of you! Culture is part of who you are! I need to help you see its importance!" ZhenZhu, who seemed to suddenly have recovered from his shock, snorted in reply. "Culture doesn't have anything to do with me! What better to sing, dance, and eat lots of food when I'm depressed, divorced, and in poverty? Such a great idea!" That statement was, of course, sarcastic.

"Perhaps we should take a ride around some of the area,". suggested Honglong steadily, before adding, "You probably should get accustomed to this place first." "Fine," hissed the grumpy janitor. Seething with disgust, he muttered, "Ben dan." Dummy in Chinese.

Heaving out a great sigh, the dragon turned to his right and swiftly glided past lakes, rivers, and trees. As they soared through the sparkling sky in silence, the dragon suddenly inquired, "How did you get divorced?" "That's private," snapped ZhenZhu, scratching his bum the whole ride. Honglong raised his fuzzy eyebrows before turning his head back towards the path. "We're getting close to destination one," he said simply. Indeed, they were slowly reaching a towering mountain, looming over them and covered head to toe with—

"Monkeys?" asked ZhenZhu, barking a laugh. Yet as the pair flew closer, there was one monkey in particular that caught their attention. It had a tiny golden helmet sitting on its head, trailing with two familiar feathers. Holding a long red stick (golden at each end) and covered with full-on glimmering body armor, it was almost impossible not to recognize the hero from the story Journey to the West. "Sun Wukong!?" ZhenZhu exclaimed, eyes popping. Creeping memories came into his mind…until he swallowed them down with a large gulp. "Precisely," said Honglong. "Or, in other words, the monkey king." As they flew past the monkeys (some of whom were snacking on peaches), Honglong explained, "Sun Wukong's rise to fame has made him loved by people alike. The poor chap was stuck in stone for a while due to punishment, so the king is thrilled with his continuing popularity." The dragon silently grinned as he watched Zhenzhu wave to the monkeys; to ZhenZhu's amazement, the monkey king himself cheerfully waved back. Even as the mountain slowly receded behind them, ZhenZhu was still looking behind him. "Don't stay looking back forever," said Honglong. "There's a whole new destination for you to see!" Slowly flying higher into the clouds, honey-sweet music filled the air with a slow, graceful melody as the pair began to see flashes of movement among the clouds. As the cotton candy clouds sluggishly floated apart, eight people came into view: one holding a paintbrush, one holding a fan, one playing the flute, one riding a donkey, one with a large calabash bottle hanging from his belt, one dancing in a large lotus flower, one holding a flower basket, one holding a green jade tablet, and one wielding an impressive sword. While (miraculously) standing on a batch of clouds, all of them were boasting, drinking, humming, and red-faced, simultaneously singing along with the flute in a merry chorus.

"Beautiful," ZhenZhu whispered. "Are these the eight immortals…?" Honglong nodded, smiling as he said, "Yes, the eight immortals who crossed the ocean. Surely you know the story?" ZhenZhu nodded, an even bigger memory resurfacing…until it was pushed back into the deeper depths of his mind. "They were drunk, right? So one of them dared that every immortal must cross the ocean in their special way, instead of traditionally using a cloud. So each of them used their objects"—he glanced at the donkey near the oldest immortal—"or animals to cross the vast ocean." "Impressive. As a person who supposedly hates your culture, you seem to know a lot about it," said the dragon in response.

Immediately the janitor's face hardened into stone, and, red-faced, he snapped, "It's common knowledge among the Chinese, alright? Just a worthless legend."

Honglong silently chastised himself for pointing that out too quickly and replied, "Ah, well, if you say so. There is a final destination that I want you to see." The glimmer from his eyes evaporated, and his scarlet scales no longer had their fierce, fiery shine. With a great huff, the wind howled and the clouds covered the view of the immortals. Zipping through the strong winds, the colorful land started to disappear. As they moved farther into the area, the willows became more withered, the ponds more polluted, and the sky darker. No longer was the hum from the waterfalls, the lullaby of the birds! Instead, the wind hissed and roared like an angered lion, while the land no longer bore fresh stalks of grass.

"What happened?" ZhenZhu demanded. The dragon only flew on, his grave baritone voice echoing throughout the dry, bitter landscape: "It will only worsen as we fly against the winds." And soon, odd, blank spots appeared, as if a magical eraser erased some of the landscape. "People are starting to doubt our culture, ZhenZhu," said Honglong, raking the dry, black dirt with his claws as they landed. "And belief is what powers this land. With more and more humans becoming invested in video games and entertainment, or experiencing harsh circumstances, they no longer love nor pay attention to the culture that was so important to their ancestors. Only popular stories and music are still thriving. But even so…" Honglong looked up, beads of large, pearl-like tears dripping down his scaly face. "Some of our world is already disappearing. In the future, even dragons will disappear, lost in memory and history."

"So people like me…caused this?" asked ZhenZhu.

Like panthers, the memories stalked into his conscience, ready to pounce. First, it started with one. He, reading Journey to the West with his children.

Then, another memory. He, telling the story of the eight immortals near the campfire.

This time, he could not stop the memories buried deep into his heart.

They rushed into his mind like a flood from the Yellow River. Him, teaching his children Chinese while they laughed and wriggled around, longing to go outside, him, making dragon puppets for his wife during New Year, singing, tradition, tang yuan, moon cakes, a new job, moving to China. The flood became bigger, punching him harder with each memory. Fighting, crying, divorce, him in China and the rest in America, longing, crying, longing, crying, going into poverty, getting a new job, moving out again, living in a stupid, broken-down hut... Loads of memories exploded into his heart like fireworks, and he suddenly remembered hugging his family as they watched the fireworks go up, up, up, then spread into the night sky like a glowing flower of different colors...reds, blues, greens, purples. Too much, too much, too much...

It was people like him who cursed this? This wasteland? Destroying this...this paradise? His fault? At first, only a single teardrop dribbled down his face, but more tears came, and before he knew it he was crying, looking up at the sky as harsh rain began to come, beating his arms, punishing him...he felt claws softly hug him, and Honglong, though looming over him like a strong, mighty giant, gave the softest of sad smiles. "I'm sorry," said ZhenZhu, shaking his head and trying to hide his silent tears. "I'm sorry for being a jerk." Honglong only nodded, his eyes shining with tears as they both cried in the rain, beautiful, glowing tears mixing with puddles on the ground. "I have felt pain too. Even after centuries of living, it is still hard to live a perfect life. Life happens. Something embarrassing, horrible, heart-breaking, it never ends. You don't need to follow every tradition in your culture, but it's still good to at least acknowledge it, and accept it as part of you, like all of our ancestors. History...is what made us." The rain began to soften as the dragon spoke these words. Before their eyes, an erased part of the land grew back, and there sprouted a tiny, single green stem. Though the effect was little, it was a start. The dragon smiled at the human, and the human smiled at the dragon. "My purpose is done now," said Honglong softly, smiling. ZhenZhu's surroundings started to blow away like bits of sand. "Wait! Will I be able to see you again?" asked ZhenZhu, the ground beginning to fall beneath his weight.

"You will," replied the dragon, haloed by new-found sunlight. "You will see me in the painting."

"Zai Jian! Goodbye!" hollered ZhenZhu as he plunged back into the human world. "Zai Jian!" Honglong hollered back, but his voice faded as the janitor's feet touched the jade floor of the temple.

ZhenZhu looked around the temple, somehow different from the time he left. Looking at the dragon painting, he could see Honglong, posed in snaky coils and reaching for the flaming pearl, yet a new feeling emerged in his heart like a rose beginning to bloom. ZhenZhu smiled, and it felt refreshing as he softly picked up his mop and bucket and headed towards the glimmering temple door. Looking back, he could see the dragon in the painting slowly look up at him...and wink.

Cultural Essay
Khanh Pham
Herbert Hoover Middle School

The journey of self-identity can claim itself to be the foundation for your life. It can be what you look up to, and build on to like brick and mortar; or it can be a forgotten house in a deep, dark alleyway. But each and every building, no matter how clandestine it proves, will one day embrace the sun. If having been stowed away and forgotten, the sun will glare, but if not then it will have learned to accept the heat. Cultures are these houses; as well as homes. Cultures are the building blocks guiding us into the world; how we were raised does play a role in how we will continue to grow. My own culture has held on to the deepest part of me, how I behave and think, and my environment has too. With both of my parents descending from Vietnam, I was raised on rice, and yes, it is the stereotypical predominant Asian household meal. But I'm here to say that I'm more than Asian; I have a melodic language that naturally rolls off my tongue, and six different tones that I can't explain no matter how many times that I try. The overlooked aspects of my own heritage are what make it unique to others.

    I feel fortunate to have inhabited a diverse community for the past years of my life. An area where others my age were respectful and aware of the many new and especially different cultures that surrounded us. Being surrounded by others who were similar but not quite the same as me has widened my vision. Just like rice; we wouldn't ever eat plain, white rice like those of different cultures might envision. Even though the majority of Asia consumes a substantial amount of rice in their lifetime, it's what goes on top of the rice that counts. Asia is the rice; but the shrimp paste and grilled pork meatballs that go on top are Vietnam.

My family had carried a piece of my hometown in Vietnam with them when they brought themselves to the United States eleven years ago. Even though we grew accustomed to the climate and constantly changing household, our traditions have remained the same. To this day, my family still eats chiffon cake with shredded meat inside, and our walls are still adorned with the exact same ancestral paintings that they did when I was two years of age. The savory flavor of my father's pho broth remains a concoction of brilliance, and the family appreciation of cuisine has risen even more since the opening of our restaurant, where we share our culture with others of the same and different.

I used to avoid elaborating about where I'm from and my daily life at home. Maybe that's due to how we have so many leafy plants around the house that flies flitted about commonly, or how we eat duck for Thanksgiving instead of turkey and mashed potatoes like the eighty-eight percent of Americans do. But all of these customs are crucial to differentiate myself from others. I've grown to accept this fact of life from the time that I was in a less diverse school during first grade and lied about the customs that guided my every step, foolishly ashamed of them. Of how they created a barrier around me that couldn't be breached; categorizing me in a different division than the rest of my friends. Of course, the regime of these thoughts didn't last for too long. The clouds that formed during my earliest stages of my mind development precipitated eventually; and I was glad that they did at a younger stage. Otherwise, I might not have the mindset I do today, when my mind is, yet, still growing.

However impactful culture can be, it doesn't have to have to linger anywhere near the realm of achievement or chance of success. I believe that if I didn't embrace my culture as it was, then I would be shadowing a fraction of myself for the rest of my life, and that could've detained my personal growth. But in terms of how culture plays a role in accomplishment, or even effort? No; we are speaking of nonexistent terms, because my culture is not my definition, and neither is it anybody else's. Neither am I a fixed definition; I am a combination of sweet and savory, meat cakes and hard work. At the end of the day, culture does influence you, and even though my Vietnamese heritage has promoted me to grow and blossom in branches that extend in different directions than those of my peers, my tree still shares a similarity with those of everyone else's; a solid trunk and limbs.

Untitled

Ella Zimmerman

Julius West Middle School

As you walk into the kitchen, you hear the sound of sizzling latkes knocking at your ear, and you see a glint of the Menorah in the corner of your eye. This is what Hanukkah feels like. Hanukkah is a Jewish holiday celebrated for eight nights and seven days. It takes people back in time to feel the miracle that happened over two thousand years ago.

Many Jewish families introduce Hanukkah with a story called "The Miracle that Happened for Eight Days." This story takes place in the land of Israel (a Jewish country) which King Antiochus Epiphanes then ruled. King Antiochus did not support all the traditions that the Jews practiced such as Shabat, or festivities such as Passover. He wanted people to worship him and not the Jew's holy temple. Antiochus wanted one religion to rule over where people looked, prayed, ate, and dressed the same. He was so set on what he desired that he banned the Jewish people from practicing any of their religions or going to their most holy place, their temple. Most of the Jews obeyed and stopped doing what they were told to do to save themselves, but not all. You see, there was a group of people called the Maccabees. This group was determined to get their religious privilege back. Led by a man named Matthias (who was later ruled by his son Juda), put up a fight against the king and ended up winning even though they were outnumbered. Finally getting their power back, they all went over to the temple which they sadly found all dirty and not taken care of. Preceding to clean it up they found something that was depressing. Only enough oil to light the Menorah for one night. Despite their bad luck, the Maccabees lit the candles. That's when the miracle happened. The candles stayed lit for eight nights and seven days! And that is how we Jews have the holy holiday called Hanukkah.

    Like Hanukkah, many holidays have a set of certain foods only eaten on the day(s) that the holiday is celebrated on. One of the main foods that Jewish people eat on Hanukkah is called latkes. Latkes are a kind of potato pancake that is fried in a pan that originated in Italy starting with the fried cheese. Which then led to Rabbi Kalyonymu ben Kalonymus creating them with potatoes instead of cheese in later years. Jewish people eat latkes to remind us of the miracle of the oil lasting for eight nights which is what they are cooked in. Due to their salty taste, people dip latkes in things like sour cream and applesauce to tone down the intense flavor.

    One of the other traditional foods that are eaten is sufganiyah. Sufganiyot is a jelly filled donut that is eaten for dessert on Hanukkah. This is eaten to again remind us about the miracle that happened relating with the oil which is what the donuts are cooked in.

    After dinner Jewish people play a game called Dreidel. The game is played with a wooden, glass, or plastic toy called a dreidel like its name. Chocolate coins called gelt are placed in the middle of the table for the players to get as the game goes on. On the sides of a dreidel there are Hebrew letters that determine how much gelt the player gets or gives to the middle. If you spin a Shin you put one piece in the middle. If you spin a Nun you get nothing nor do anything. If you spin a Hey you get half of the gelt in the middle. And if you spin a Gimal you get everything from the middle. Dreidel is most commonly played by children for a fun way to celebrate. These things will bring all families together to celebrate a time of happiness and joy. It means the world for all Jewish people to practice these customs and more during holy times.

       Before eating, Jewish people light something called a Hanukkiah. This is a candle holder that has nine places for each candle. Most people call it a Menorah but traditionally it is a Hanukkiah. Each night the family lights a candle in the center of the Hanukkiah. The center candle is called shamash and it is lit every night. It is then used to light the amount of candles depending on what night it is. After lighting the candles two prayers are said. This is different on the first night where people say three prayers. These prayers are thanking God for bringing us to this season from the light that has guided us to where we are today. While we say these prayers it is a time for all families to come together and cherish the moment in peace. It is a time for us to reconnect to ourselves in thanking God for guidance of life to the point we are now. We look forward to the years to come while looking back at the past and cherishing the memories that were made, and also the hard times that we pushed through to make it here. We also thank ourselves for never giving up and following our path in mind, body and spirit. And most importantly we thank our loved ones for sticking by your side through all of the things that life made hard. We then come back to the present and look forward for the times to come and the things that we will accomplish.

As I feel that we have no choice but to conclude it has been a wonderful experience to look back on Hanukkah. It is a holiday that will stick with us for many years to come. It is so amazing that people all over the world celebrate like shown. As I retire this journey I wanted to say that you should always be proud of who you are. No matter what your customs are or what you celebrate, it all has an impact on the world and maybe just even a friend to sit down and share about it.

My Culture
Kristian Carpenter
Eastern Middle School

I've spent the majority of my life living a lie. No one ever asked, so I figured it would be better to be discreet, almost when it came to my culture. It was as if my culture was like an annoying fly that was following me, haunting me. I thought that culture was only about race and where you came from.

However, I couldn't ignore my culture forever. In 5th grade, we had an assignment about race. We were to make a poster about where we're from. Of course, being me, I didn't want to do America. I was sure that since my skin color was black, I was from Ethiopia, Lagos, or elsewhere in Africa. That day, I talked to my parents, and they told me that my Uncle had taken a test on Ancestry to find out his roots and that since I am related to him, I might be able to find something. While calling him, I found out he is mixed and made up of multiple races. I looked over all of them and decided to choose Nigeria. After much research, I made my poster and brought it to school to present. Many people were confused as to if I was Nigerian because my twin sister was American, but no one bothered to ask me. Yet, people don't care that much in middle school.

It was my first week of school, and I was in 7th period media class. We were doing an icebreaker on your favorite food, so I decided to talk to the two Ethiopian girls sitting next to me. One of the girls first said to me, "I like cheese". But the second thing she said I knew would change me forever.

"Where are you from," she said.

My first instinct was to say "Oh, I'm from Cincinnati!" but I knew exactly what she was thinking. She was thinking, "Where are you from in Africa?" Nevertheless, I said I was from Cincinnati like I would to anyone asking me where I was from. I remember her immediately saying afterward, "No, I mean where are you really from?". The other girl sitting next to her added: "Yeah, like where are you from in Africa?" I sat silently in my seat for a minute before answering: "I'm from Nigeria." I instantly regret it after saying it. I knew I wasn't really from Nigeria, or at least I wasn't born in Nigeria. She responded with a simple "You don't look Nigerian. You look, like, Somalian or something. After that, she started asking me what type of hair I had, and after telling her I had 4c hair, she again responded with "No, you don't." I started to ask her why she thought that, but we were interrupted by the teacher to start the next lesson. When the bell rang later to end the class, I stopped the girl and asked her why she had thought that I didn't have 4c hair. She explained that her friend had 4c hair and that her braids were usually much chunkier than mine looked. I told her that my hair had been blow-dried before being braided and walked away. That same girl is now one of my friends, but we fight a lot. The 2nd girl is now one of my very close friends. But it didn't end there.

A few weeks ago, one of my Ethiopian friends started calling me a monkey. At first, I was cool with it because she didn't do it much, and maybe it was only because we were close enough for her to call me that. But the more she started doing it, the more frustrated I would get about it. Soon, she took it too far and told me I wasn't black because I wasn't from Africa. It took me so long to explain to everyone that I was black, and I even had to bring up Beyonce and how her parents are from America, too. Eventually, it died down and I forgave Lilian, but a lot of my friends still say offensive stuff sometimes.

But all of these events lead up to who I am now, positive or negative. When I found out about this contest, I was convinced I wouldn't be able to even try because I didn't know what my culture was, but I do now. My culture is how I style my hair. My culture is the type of clothing I wear. My culture is my singing voice, my cello experience, and even how I write.

My culture is me.

The Sum of My Values
Reya Ganesh
Hallie Wells Middle School

Indira Nooyi: Beacon of leadership and CEO of PepsiCo. Dr. APJ Abdul Kalam: Famous scientist known as "The Missile Man." Sachin Tendulkar: The only batsman to score 100 centuries, thereby known as "The God of Cricket." What do all these people have in common? They are each from humble beginnings, linked to the diverse country of India. It is where I too am from—at least my parents. Like Nooyi, my parents and our primogenitors were born in the southeastern state of Tamil Nadu; thus, my mother tongue is Tamil, the oldest language still spoken. Various things make up the traditions of this state, but living abroad, many of my customs are closer to those of the United States. However, I still celebrate the patterns of Indian praxis festivals, engage in their dances, and avail myself of the food. Together, these are the sum of my values.

Everyone has their own culture that defines their mode of living. My parents still celebrate the cultures of their youth with the community here, but they can never be as extravagant as the ones back in their homeland. Similarly, those from other parts of the world have their own traditions. My culture is a blend of those of my family and those of the land in which I live. A vital part of this is the gatherings.

Snap. Snap. SNAP! Diwali, or Deepavali–derived from the Sanskrit word dipavli meaning "rows of lights"–as is the term in Tamil, is the festival of lights. Fireworks boom and snap in the night sky as we celebrate this paramount festival. It is when light conquers over darkness, whereupon knowledge trounces ignorance, and consequently good vanquishes evil. Nationwide, this fete won't be taken without celebration, easily identifiable by the burning clay lamps (diya), special decorations, puja (prayers), and the gatherings of families for which a feast with the company of sweets ensues. I feel content lighting fireworks with my family and friends. Analogously, particular regions have their own rituals. The four days of Pongal—Bhogi Pongal, Surya Pongal, Mattu Pongal, and Kaanum Pongal—compose a multi-day harvest festival that takes place in the month of Thai in the Tamil solar calendar, usually commencing on the 14th or 15th of January. I celebrate this festival and enjoy wishing my grandparents on this special occasion. These are some of the many festivals that result in a happy gathering and sometimes mixes of cultures. I recognize many Indian celebrations and others, such as Christmas, my parents have grown up with. I am also aware of those that necessitate countywide holidays in America, but they often don't carry the same feeling as those special to my whole family. A chance for people to congregate is crucial anywhere, especially since relatives are widespread throughout the country. Staying awake until midnight on New Year's Eve is a testament to the deep bonds of friends we call siblings, and that is akin to many. Fetes are also times to entertain and to show off; one way to do both is by dancing.

Tap. Tap. Tap. The beating of my feet against the cold, hard floor produces a loud noise to keep the beat. I look right and left, up and down at my hands as I hurry to keep up with the pace with meaningful facial expressions. Dance is another way I can express my cultural identity. I do Bharatanatyam, a classical dance that originated in Tamil Nadu. Bharatnatyam is one of the nine Indian classical dance forms that the Sangeet Natak Akademi recognizes. It includes a great mix of South Indian religious themes, particularly Shaivism and Hinduism (Lord Shiva is considered the god of this dance). Along with Kuchipudi, it is among the toughest classical dance forms in India for its complex steps, hand gestures, and intense facial expressions. This and freestyle dancing with Indian songs allow me to express my culture at gatherings. Ensuingly, I connect with both the people in my group and those of others to make new boon companions. Dance serves as a mode of exercise, a way to learn rhythm, a means to learn history through culture, and, principally, a way to have fun. Dance and entertainment are an imperative part of any gathering, but as many will agree, you can't have a gala without the food.

The spice of my idli and podi searing my tongue, but for which my tongue is unsatiated. The sweetness of the kaju katli makes my taste buds dance with joy. The pure jubilation of biryani, for which I can eat the lion's share. Rightfully so, India is characterized by its spices. Even when he founded America, Christopher Columbus' original endeavor was to discover a new spice trade route to connect with India. But spices don't encompass the whole palate. Sweet. Salty. Sour. Bitter. Umami. The variety of tastes appeals to people's taste buds all over the world. New combinations have sprung up even in recent times. Food is an enormous part of my culture, and though diets vary in different regions, even within India itself, it will invariably remain an often pleasurable need of survival.

Many things make up culture, including music, art, food, philosophy, religion, and literature, but they are mixed easily with the manners of others. I watch Tamil cinema, wear Indian clothing when going to temples or on auspicious dates, and do many other things necessitated by my culture. Guests are treated with the utmost politeness, and it is the common belief that any food containers are returned and refilled. But I am also part American in that I wear the clothing, speak the language, and even have a passport from the country. My parents have brought over many of their traditions from India, but they know it is best to adapt to the growing world. Cultural mixing is already in full swing; however, whether it will hurt or hinder posterity remains unknown. Still, a blend of new ideas is always welcome for growing theories. My culture is important to me, and although I can only somewhat understand my mother tongue, I reap the benefits of visiting the place of my parents' birth and trying to understand my ancestors even in their old age. Everyone's norms are different, and mine are intrinsically linked to both the beautiful countries of India and America.

Outsider
Madeleine Lee
Thomas W. Pyle Middle School

I am different
I feel like an outsider
They exclude me
Pretend I am not there
Even when they clearly acknowledge me

Is it because of what I look like?
Where I come from?
The way I speak?
The way I act?
What I say?

I am cast aside
Forgotten
And yet I don't know why
Tell me

Is there a reason for this injustice?
Or are they doing this for "fun"
Because I don't feel like laughing

When I walk by, they whisper
When I sit down, they move away
When I ask a question, they roll their eyes

Does anyone care?

I do
Will anyone put an end to their hate?
I hope

I am different
Seen as an outsider
I know I am like them on the inside
And someday I will be seen for who I am
That I am sure of.

Culture Poems
Aria Roy
Francis Scott Key Middle School

Poem #1

Land of a thousand hues, India,
Diverse cultures and traditions, a
Cornucopia
A tapestry woven with threads of unity,
Embracing differences with grace and
dignity.

From the snow-capped peaks of the
Himalayas,
To the sun-kissed beaches of the
Andaman Bay,
The land exudes a charm that's hard to ignore,
A land that has always been adorned by
Folklore,

The mystic rhythms of sitar and tabla,
The vibrant hues of silk and cotton and saris,
The aroma of spices that fill the air,
A tapestry of sounds, smells, and colors to
Ensnare.
Temples and mosques, churches and
gurudwaras,
Sacred rivers and hold rocks, invoking the
Gods,

A land where devotion and faith coexist,
A land where the Divine is present in every
Midst.

A land of festivals, of joy, and mirth
A place where celebrations are away
Of life on earth,
A land of timeless beauty and grandeur,
A land that forever remains an enigma to the world's
explorers.

India, a land of a billion hearts,
A place where love and compassion never
departs,
A land that embraces all with open arms,
A land that has always been the epitome
Of calm

Poem #2

India and Bangladesh, two lands of
Wonder,
Their cultures and traditions, a tapestry of
splendor,
From the Himalayas to the Bay of Bengal,
Their diversity and beauty, forever to
Entangle.

The sarees and bangles of India,
The lungis and saris of Bangladesh,
Their clothing, an expression of their
Heritage,

And the uniqueness that sets them apart.

The rhythms of the tabla and dhol,
The melodies that touch our soul,
The music and dance of these lands,
A symphony of joy that expands.

The curries and biryanis of India,
The pithas and samosas of Bangladesh,
The food of these nations, a treat for all,
A feast for taste buds, a gastronomic call.

The people of India and Bangladesh,
Warm and welcoming, with hearts to Match,
Generosity and kindness in their veins,
Their love for others, never-ending Refrain.
So let us celebrate these cultures,
Their art., their music, their literature,
For they are unique and beautiful ,
A treasure that will last forevermore

Pongal - The Tamil Thanksgiving
Dilshan Prakash
Hallie Wells Middle School

As I looked out of the train's window bars, I saw a desert of orange dust with sharp rocks scattered all around. Occasionally I would spot peacocks wandering around, seeming out of place with its bright blue feathers. Then the landscape gradually changed and I would see lush green fields getting harvested by hand. I came to India for winter break, and since my parents wanted to celebrate Pongal - the harvest festival, in their homeland, they extended our vacation. So for the last 3 weeks we visited places in and around Chennai, the capital of Tamil Nadu. Tamil Nadu is a state in India. Tamil, my mother tongue, is the official language of Tamil Nadu. On the last week of our India trip, we were traveling to Madurai, a city in Southern Tamil Nadu. Madurai is where my great-grandma, who is 89 years old, lived throughout her life. Along with our visit to our great-grandma, Pongal - the festival of harvest, was also just starting tomorrow, January 14. My mom used to say that Pongal celebration would be more lively in Madurai than Chennai. So here I was, on a train reaching the outskirts of Madurai.

When we left the train station, I saw a very strange bird. It was tall and gray. When I asked my mom (In Tamil, "amma") what it was, she replied it was a female peacock(peahen). She also explained that only male peacocks have colorful feathers. We took an Auto Rickshaw (

a type of taxi) to drop us off at my great-grandma's house. I wasn't shocked when the ride cost us around 1000 rupees; I understood it was about $12 due to the exchange rate. As we went, we passed by a market bustling with people buying everything they needed to celebrate Pongal. The shops selling sugarcane, claypots, turmeric roots and garlands were overcrowded. The colors of goods and attire, the aroma of spices, the sound of bargaining shoppers made the marketplace more vibrant. When we reached my great-grandma's house, we were greeted with welcomes and compliments from my great-grandma (In Tamil, "patti") and a few more relatives who were with her. Everyone was happy to see that I could talk in Tamil. They were getting ready for the Pongal celebration, whether it was buying ingredients for preparing dishes, distributing new clothes and decorating the house with some types of leaves and many colorful, fragrant flowers. After a whole day of train travel, I felt exhausted so went to bed early.

The next morning was the first day of Pongal. My dad woke me up abruptly. "Wake up. Today is Pongal." I looked at the antique clock on the wall. It was 5:30 AM. I felt a bit agitated at first, but as I heard the noises of the festivities, I slowly got up. He continued, "Today is the day to offer our prayers to the sun, so get ready. Also, wear the traditional dress that patti gave to you", pointing to the new dhoti(an Indian dress) and velvet and sparkling shirt on the table near me. As I brushed my teeth with the bitter toothpaste, I saw my mom, and many relatives were drawing "kolams". A Kolam is a symmetrical design drawn near a house entrance on special occasions. When my mom said "The space at home limits how much you could celebrate," she was right. For one thing, the kolams in India seem to be much bigger. When I went outside, I saw a rainbow of colorful kolams near the gate. In the center, I saw a small gas stove. I politely asked my "achappa" (grandpa), "Why is there a stove?" He hastily replied "That is for cooking pongal." and rushed away. The festival and the main dish made for celebration share the same name - "Pongal". The best part of the Pongal festival day is cooking the pongal dish. Pongal dish is prepared by boiling rice with milk seasoned with nuts and jaggery (a type of cane sugar).

As I thought about how delicious the pongal dish would be for my empty stomach, my great-grandma called to me "come over here!" When I dashed near the stove, I found two sugarcane stalks were now leaning on near the stove and the pongal dish was almost overflowing, just as the sun rose. When it finally spilled over the rim of the clay pot, we all shouted "Pongalo pongal!". It means "Let it overflow". The contextual meaning is "to be blessed with abundance all year around". We offered our prayers to thank the sun and nature for the harvest. It was so delicious to eat pongal for breakfast on a banana leaf. My grandpa cut a piece of sugarcane and gave it to me. It was fun to bite and peel the sugarcane and suck the sugary juice.

The second day of Pongal is "Mattu" Pongal. "Mattu" means "cow". That day was dedicated to cows which were helpful to the farmers. Since my great-grandma didn't have any, we didn't celebrate it at home. However, my mom still drew a kolam depicting a few cows. We went to a temple to offer prayers and then traveled to a town called Alanganallur. We rode through a scenic road winding through coconut farms. After a 30 minute drive, we reached my grandma's younger sister's house. I respectfully greeted them and entered their living room. The living room was barren except for the T.V and huge, ancient swing made out of pure teak wood passed on from generations. I jumped on and began swinging away till it began creaking. It was fun to push the swing to its limits. However, when I jumped off, I got hit by the swing. Although it was going pretty slow, it hurt a lot just because it was huge and heavy. In the evening, my grandpa gave us a surprise. He got us tickets to see a "Jallikattu" event. The "Jallikattu" is a contest, where people try to grab a small bag full of prize money from the horn of a bull.

Once I got to the stadium, I saw that all the contestants were wearing red just to agitate the bull. "Poor bull," my sister sighed when she saw the crowd waiting to catch the bull. All the players were anxiously waiting at the door for the wild bull to be released. All of a sudden the narrow door opened, and a big bull with a bump for a shoulder ran into the arena. As it ran, a contestant grabbed its hump and clung onto it for dear life. However, the bull jumped and swung him away like a cannon. It stood in the middle of the field, turning at whoever made the slightest move. When someone threw a cloth at it, it acted up again, running at the cloth and the poor person who was standing there. As he backed away, he tripped into the dust and just as the bull tried to impale him with its horns, another person grabbed the money bag tied to its horn. The bull changed its attention and knocked him over, but it was too late. The players had won the prize.

For dinner, we had an Indian street food called "kothu parotta" from a street vendor. The name means minced Indian bread and it is served with gravy. It was very delicious on a chilly day back in America. However, for me, it wasn't great in warm weather.

The last day of Pongal is "Kaanum" Pongal. "Kaanum" means "Seeing". On this day, we meet relatives and friends. We also planned for an extended family get-together. Since it was a Pongal holiday for everyone in Tamil Nadu, many of my relatives came. The first people to join were my close relatives whom I meet often in India, like my cousins and grandma who lived nearby. For the gathering, everyone was wearing their best clothing. When more distant relatives came, my cousins introduced their families. Me and my cousins rocked the swing until it began creaking, acting like it was a giant ship and the floor were jagged rocks. Then, when we scouted the 2nd floor, we found a small, "hidden" staircase and another room that was very dusty and unfurnished. Then, we went up to the balcony and tried a few herbs and peppers. Although I was the best in withstanding the bitterness of the Neem leaf, I was too scared to eat the peppers. Kavin, my mom's- cousins son, won the spice competition by a landslide by eating a pepper without any water.

After our adventures, we went back to the swing and watched television for some time. Then we had a lunch feast of chicken gravy, goat leg curry, fish fry, chicken biryani, naan (Indian bread), and yogurt. We had a lot of mouth watering non veg dishes for Kaanum-pongal. Being me, I enjoyed all my favorites - biryanis and frys. Around evening all the relatives started to leave. Suddenly I heard my mom's voice - "Have dinner and get ready for bed. Tomorrow early morning we have to go to Madurai and catch the train to Chennai."

The next morning, as we started our train journey back to Chennai I started recollecting my Pongal celebration memories. As I thought about the cousins we met and the fun we had, it reminded me of my friends back home in the USA. It's been a while since we all met. I felt a bit sad missing my friends for a long time. When did we last meet? Suddenly a thought flashed. The U.S have an American version of Pongal. It's Thanksgiving! The dress we wear or the food we make for these festivals are way different. The Thanksgiving turkey is very different from the sweet pongal dish in many aspects. But I see the purpose of both the festivals are very similar. The harvest and gathering together. Suddenly, I grasped onto something even more important. The reason why they both exist is to spend time with family and friends and appreciate nature. After this, I understood why it was so good to have both cultures as part of me. I had two festivals each year to enjoy with my family and friends and to thank nature. To me, Pongal is Tamil Thanksgiving and Thanksgiving is an American Pongal.

7th Grade
Winners & Honorable Mentions

Where Do I Fit In?
Juno Seigel
Eastern Middle School

What's your culture? A seemingly simple question that arouses complexities for me. Where do I fit in? It's hard to explain. My dad is Jewish, but we don't go to a synagogue, and my mom is Atheist. Although my family on my dad's side gathers for some of the holidays such as Passover and Yom Kippur sometimes, we don't do many other things, like pray. But here's where it gets complicated: my mom is half Chinese, which means we also celebrate Chinese New Year, making dumplings and getting little red envelopes. And to make things even more tricky, now, because my stepmom celebrates Christmas, my dad, brother, and I do too. Which leads me to wonder: what is my culture?

If my mom was Jewish, I might be able to say I was Jewish, since in the Jewish culture the religion is passed down from the mother's side. But it's my dad's side. While all my Jewish friends are studying for their bat or bar mitzvah, the only Hebrew I know is the beginning of the Hanukkah prayer. If I wanted to go to Israel for free, as a part of the Birthright, would I be allowed? I grew up in a household that celebrated Hanukkah, and I loved lighting the candles with my brother as a kid. We would eat latkes and play Dreidel on special occasions. But that doesn't necessarily make me Jewish, does it? Usually, when someone asks me my religion, I just say that I'm Jewish, because it's just easier that way. Yet is that accurate?

When I tell people I'm a quarter Chinese, they usually don't believe me. "Are you sure you're not just White?" "You don't look Chinese." It's not a big deal, and it doesn't bother me that much, because after all I'm only a quarter Chinese. My grandma, who is Chinese and grew up in Taiwan, lived with me and my family for about 10 years of my childhood. She would babysit my older brother and I sometimes, and during those times she would tell me folktales. Not only Chinese folktales, but Hawaiian ones as well. She would also teach me some of the Buddhist stories, and occasionally I would have tea or meditate with her. Is this sufficient practice to be a part of Chinese culture? How do I know when I am part of a certain culture?

I never celebrated Christmas until my stepmom came into my life. She's not religious either, but she loves the whole idea of stockings and pine trees and Christmas in general. So when she and my dad began dating about a year and some after my parents got divorced, we began celebrating Christmas as well. I didn't go to church or anything, but we exchanged presents. But wait, there's more. Before my stepmom, my family would celebrate New Years as a gift exchanging holiday. We would each write one another pretty lengthy letters about the past year and how grateful we were for each other. Even after we began celebrating Christmas, we never stopped our New Year's custom. I love that tradition, but in my opinion it just doesn't make sense. Why should we celebrate a holiday, exchange gifts, then five days later just get more gifts? I love the idea of Christmas, and I love giving and receiving gifts, but is there a point at which it's just too much? I feel like it should be spaced out a bit, because one week seems too soon.

In conclusion, my culture is everything from the smoke of the Hanukkah candles to my grandma's homemade quiche, from marches and rallies to my soccer team's traditional "Secret Soccer Sisters", from pumpkin pancakes to the talk of a new book in my English class, or new choreography in Drama. Every new tradition that I begin, every new group of friends I make. Even though I don't have a set culture, my culture is not limited to one thing, and it is something that I can decide for myself, even though all my interactions certainly influence it.

Split
Jitu Abebe
Silver Creek Middle School

I am split
Split between two worlds
So similar, yet so different nonetheless

My world outside
Is full of trends
And fast fashion
And lighter skin

Full of expensive styles
And cringy jokes
And stereotypes
Within

Full of unspoken rules
And weird norms
And rumors that make me spin

My world outside
Is full of people unknown, yet known nonetheless
And strict teachers
And loads of work
That only causes more stress
And rigorous classes
And competitive classmates
That all dream

Of success

My world outside
Is full
Of people that I love dearly
Friends that feel like siblings
That I care about
Sincerely

Their bright smiles and hearty laughs
Like the sun on a cloudy day
Lure me closer and closer
To my world outside
Pulling me in instead of away

And as I subconsciously try to comply
And step into their world
Into my world outside
I realize their differences
And pull away
Hesitation filling me
Knowing they've already chosen to stay
While I
Am split

And torn
Between my world outside
And my world
The one I was created in
Raised in
Not exposed to

The world
At home
And at church
With my close friends

Whose chocolate skin resembles mine
Whose hair shrinks and bounces like springs
That clump and combine

Whose slang matches up with mine
And whose personalities align
With the one I have to confine
In my world outside

The world
With long, white dresses
And stunning head scarfs with a range of intricate designs
And different foods that seem "odd" to my world outside
But are so, very, divine

The world
With playful and romantic music
That drums in my ears
Mixing Amharic and English into one perfect melody
As I dance away with laughs and cheers
To dances
From **both** of my worlds

The world with my family
So strongly connected to their roots
The roots that grasp my leg and beg me to stay
When I'm tempted to join my world outside

Filling me with fond memories that hold me down
And pull me back as I try to step in
Keeping me split

This world is what I consider
My world

And as much as I love
My world outside
And my own world too
It's difficult to be part of both

Because when you're held down by invisible binds
That no one seems to see but you
And unlimited temptations
That **sometimes**, you want to pursue
It becomes a struggle to completely step into one world
When you long for the other too

Yet in these two worlds
So similar, yet different nonetheless
The fact remains
That the one thing I wish for
Is something I might never obtain

The only way I can
Is to make my choice
And break the roots and binds that ground me to each world
Until I can take a step into the one I **choose** to be in
And become **whole**

But as much as I yearn
To be whole
And finally complete
I know
That stepping into one world
Means **letting go** of the other

And so
In fear
And in doubt
I let these shackles bind me
And these roots confine me

And as I dangle my legs
On the edge of these two worlds
I remain
Split

The Fortune Cookies
Sofia Ou
Eastern Middle School

The time of the Chinese New Year was when the house was decorated with red lanterns that glowed soothingly, being rocked back and forth by the chilly fists of the wind. It was almost night, but not yet. When it was night, the celebration would begin. It was the only red-dressed house in America compared to the others, which were gray and plain.

The house's large windows were decorated with scarlet paper cuttings that read "福," which meant luck. The tall, polished wooden door had paper door banners, filled with rich crimson red and gold brimming around the corners. Behind the door, there lived a girl Vivian Li, who was not too excited.

Chinese New Year was supposed to be spiritful, but Vivian sighed, feeling spiritless. Her parents had bickered at each other for each mistake. Her Mama complained, "AIYA! We have to impress the aunties and uncles! I see a speck of dust! How dirty! Squeaky clean for good luck, you see! Or bad spirits would come to us!" Her Baba murmured, "You seem to be the bad spirit, lah. I can't see how we can enjoy the food on burnt dumplings, haiyah." Vivian said, "Calm down! This is about family, which is more important than food and cleaning." Her parents continued complaining to each other, ignoring her. Vivian wished she could solve this problem. But she knew how to solve this. Vivian put on her scarlet coat, boots, and hat. She slid a lucky red envelope into her pocket, rushed out of the door, and ran to the little koi fish pond, where she usually found the "Fortune Cookie Lady". After a few minutes of searching, Vivian spotted the Fortune Cookie Lady, who was always strolling around with a cart filled with fortune cookies. With determination pumped in Vivian's veins, she skidded towards Fortune Cookie Lady and panted, "Ni hao, hello, may I get some fortune cookies from you?" The Fortune Cookie Lady was dressed in different hues and shades of red, and gold in the rims and hems of the clothing, golden pictures of the twelve zodiacs pouncing around stitched into the robes. The Fortune Cookie Lady, face shaped like the moon and wrinkles like the ripples in a pond, smiled at the girl and asked, "Why do you want my fortune cookies so badly?"

Her white hair outshined the shiniest of silver and jade, and her eyes twinkled like gold.

Vivian replied, "Well, my Mama and Baba are arguing over petty things. All they want to do every Chinese New Year is to impress the aunties and uncles with the "perfect" decorations and "perfect" food. I want to show them that family is the true meaning of Chinese New Year, so I want to give them fortune cookies to cheer them up." The Fortune Cookie Lady's eyes glinted even more, and she said, "Oh, I have the perfect batch of fortune cookies to solve this problem!" She grabbed a bag of fortune cookies with her wrinkled dried dates fingers and plopped them in Vivian's hands. The Fortune Cookie Lady advised, "When you break open a fortune cookie, inside it, the paper tells you fun places to do or go to. It will help you and your family bond together even more, and you will have the happiest Chinese New Year! Happy joyous year of the dragon!" Excited, Vivian took out her red envelope and inquired, "How much for the fortune cookies?" The old lady shook her head and said, "The fortune cookies are for free! It is Chinese New Year so you and your family will discover the true meaning of Chinese New Year."

Vivian shook with sheer excitement, gently grabbing the bag of fortune cookies. "Thank you so much, Fortune Cookie Lady! Have a Happy New Year!" Before Vivian left, the Fortune Cookie Lady yelled, "Wait! I have something else to give you!" Just as Vivan gave a glance, the golden dragon, who was once resting on the Fortune Cookie Lady's dress, escaped and was filled with life, pouncing and breathing with fire. Then more animals appeared, Rat, Ox, Tiger, Rabbit, Snake, Horse, Goat, Monkey, Rooster, Dog, and Pig. All of them were zodiacs. The Rat patted its fat belly and squeaked, "May I have a fortune cookie, too? I am starving!" Vivian, shocked at first, soon smiled. "This…is so cool! I was born in the year of the Dragon, and I'm turning twelve! This is why there are twelve zodiac signs! My Mom is a Goat and my Dad is the year of the Horse!" In reply, the Goat bleated a "BaaaaAa!" and the horse neighed elegantly, hooves kicking into the air, dark mane swishing and dancing with the wind. "Thanks again, Fortune Cookie Lady, now follow me, Zodiacs!" cried Vivan joyfully as she rushed towards her home.

She peered through the windows of her house, parents still bickering, not noticing she was gone for a bit. She turned to the Zodiacs and said, "You guys, stay here for a bit.

Wait for me." Then she huffed in a sigh, opened the door, and went in. "Mama, Baba," Vivian quipped as she interrupted the arguing, "Do you guys want some fortune cookies?" Mama and Baba turned to look at Vivian, glanced at each other, and then nodded. They sat on the red family couch where the TV's screen was filled with operas, dancing…and happy families. Happy families who cared about family, and nothing else. The zodiacs were still peering in through the windows, but her parents didn't notice. Vivian watched keenly as Mama and Baba unwrapped the crispy cookies, and CRUNCH, broke the fortune cookie into two pieces. Mama took the piece of paper from her fortune cookie and read out loud, "Make shadow puppets from paper…this is no ordinary fortune cookie, it doesn't say my future!" Meanwhile, Baba took his piece of paper from his cracked fortune cookie and read aloud, "Go to the Chinese New Year Parade with a dancing dragon costume…hmm…" Vivian took a fortune cookie and CRUNCH. She opened her fortune cookie and the paper flew out like a phoenix. She read from the paper: "Watch the fireworks with your family, as family is the most important." Tears welled up in her eyes as the words spilled from Vivian's mouth like a fountain.

      Her Mama and Baba looked at her sincerely and patted her on the back. "Vivian, it sounds like a great idea, but I don't know if we have time to make shadow puppets. Maybe spend more time studying…" her Mama said. "Yeah," her Baba joined in, "The Chinese New Year parade is too far away from our house, and do we even have a dragon costume? Vivi, you know how costumes and that rubbish make my wallet sob and scream, hiyah! So expensive! But the fortune cookies are really tasty…" But then…CRASH! The zodiacs flew through the windows, shattering it. "Don't worry!" roared the Dragon, "My fast powers can take you to the parade! And you don't need a dragon costume, you already have me!" Snake said, "I already made puppets with my speediness, and I can control all of them at once. Well, depends if you like hastily made puppets made from wood, leaves, and mud…" The Rabbit said, "I and the other Zodiacs can create the fireworks! It would be so fun!" The Rat complained, "When can I have a fortune cookie?"

    Vivian looked at her parents, but they had already fainted, faces as pale as parchment. The Dragon snickered. "Pfft…we can still carry the mortals on my backs, asleep or not. Come on! Hop on!" Before Vivian jumped on, she grabbed the remaining fortune cookies. Ox and Monkey had to heave her parents onto the impatient Dragon's back, but when the deed was done, the Dragon lifted off, the animals pursuing and following him. As they were in the sky, Vivian saw a long stream of thundering red and gold, sparkling here and there. "This must be the parade!" remarked Vivian. "Let's go down!" The Dragon, following Vivian's orders descended, where people were cheering, and people were dancing, wearing lion costumes that varied from green to red to yellow and more. By then, Vivian's parents had already woken up. Vivian's Baba was the first to blink his eyes open. He remarked, "WHAT JUST HAPPENED! OH NO! PARTY IS GOING TO START IN 4 HOURS, AIYAH!" Her Mama twitched from the loud yelling, eyes wide and concerned. She screeched, "I saw a whole farm of animals! What was that all about? And a dragon too? Oh please let's go back home, my boiled fish gonna turn into failure clumps after all the heat!"

Vivian reassuredly patted them on the backs. "Guys, what matters is that we can do fun stuff in the parade. Now let's join in!"

Her Baba blurted, "I will forgive you if you get 100% on every test, but you never do!"

Her Mama agreed, "Yes, Vivian, remember that one quiz where you got a 95%? That was such a disappointment. Also, the lowest score you got on a quiz was 91. A 91! You were close to a dreadful B! Luckily you didn't, or else my ancestors would have been shedding tears of anguish. "

Vivian rolled her eyes. Instead of family, her parents were blabbering on about grades.

The Dog, who barked, and Pig who oinked, shoved the parents and Vivian into the parade, the Dragon whooshing after Vivian. Vivian's ears caught the surprised remarks from people like a fisherman catching salmon. "Wow! That Dragon costume is realistic," a child peeped to his mother, "Mama, can I have a Dragon costume like that too?"

The lion dancers, curious, circled Vivian, her parents, and the Dragon, admiring with oohs and ahs. The Dragon was a remarkable dancer, as he flitted his great tail around, and stomped, scales strident against the sun, soon fading into the moon. The Dragon lifted his scaly face to the sky and breathed flames, a girl squeaking, "I didn't know dragon costumes could breathe fire!" While monkey used Dragon's fire to light the firecrackers, making the firecrackers explode into fiery flowers. People clapped at the beautiful fireworks that danced around.

The Dragon wasn't the only zodiac having fun. Tiger was curious about the "Lions" dancing in the parade. Snake showed the children the puppets, Ox was giving rides, and Rooster was getting chased by a fat cat, and all seemed well. Even Vivian's parents were having fun, bit by bit. This was Vivian's best Chinese New Year. She was finally showing her parents that family was the most important when celebrating the holidays. After spending three hours having fun, snacking on rice cakes, honey-covered fruits, (and more fortune cookies!) Vivian's parents remembered that the party they hosted was in one hour.

Vivian hugged her parents and looked at the dragon with a thankful smile. "Can you take us home?" She asked the scaly creature who breathed fire. The dragon nodded. Vivian and her parents hopped onto the dragon's spiny back. The dragon launched into the sky, the rest of the zodiacs trailing behind.

When they arrived at the house, it seemed happier. Sadly, the zodiacs departed, each one giving a special hug to Vivian, returning to the magical Fortune Cookie Lady. Vivian was left with her parents, and she felt unmeasurable happiness inside of her. She and her parents played games and helped prepare the delicious feast until the guests arrived, family and friends, the ones that mattered. The feast was excitable as ever, but not the same without the zodiacs. I wonder if my next Chinese New Year would be similar to this, Vivian thought to herself. Families in the party, chittered and chattered and Vivian heard one of her Aunties wonder out loud, "I wonder why that window is broken…"

 While people were busy feasting, Vivian opened another fortune cookie with a big CRUNCH. Then the paper flew out. The fortune cookie wrote, "In the Next Chinese New Year it will be like this too, after all, your family and friends will always stay with you."

The End

Biryani-Lessons
Sufyana Johnson
Westland Middle School

Every Friday after Jummah prayer, the community streams gradually out of the masjid, chatting and catching up with various friends and acquaintances. Being a heavy-duty chatter means remaining in the mosque, talking to the imam long after everyone else is outside (then, once outside, talking to many, many, many more people). Being a chatter's daughter means countless people whose faces are barely recognizable to you asking, "Salaam-Alaikum, where is your mother? Is she here?" It means having to explain, "Walaikum-Salaam, yes, she's here, she's still inside, though she said she was coming out about 10 minutes ago, but she most likely has forgotten about that by now." Not being a chatter, however, means you get to be first in line to get biryani in the food line outside, maybe some chickpeas (or "chickadees" as my two-year-old sister calls them) if they're there, and then finding some obscure bench by the basketball courts to share your biryani with said little sister. (Then, fifteen minutes later, walking back inside to find your mother still chatting away.)

Every person in my family will eat biryani, even my other little sister, who is ten-years-old and who proclaims everything from dahl to samosas to chicken curry to be 'too spicy.' Biriyani is there at nearly every Jummah that we manage to go to, and has been at so many parties at family friend's houses, and at our community gatherings like weddings and birth celebrations and funerals. Because of this, it's surprising that my family doesn't make it more often. My mother made it once, to celebrate New Year's a couple years back, but until recently I hadn't made it at all.

The Hunger Van is a program that my masjid runs, where trays of fruit, salad, and biryani are made and delivered to local homeless shelters. I signed up to be a Hunger Van volunteer to earn some student service learning hours. I arrived on time, but due to bad weather, I was the first volunteer there. Foolishly, I answered 'yes' to the question, "Do you know how to cook?" posed by the friendly person in charge, not knowing what I would be cooking, and found myself suddenly assigned, along with a seventeen-year-old boy who had showed up, to the making of chicken biryani.

It was a little embarrassing admitting that I had eaten biryani a bunch of times but had no idea how to wash or cook rice other than Rice-A-Roni, but the washing was over in a couple of minutes, not including the du'aa that happened once everyone finally arrived, the gist of it being the simple asking of God to bless those less fortunate than us. That's a very core belief in Islam, zakat* being one of the five pillars every Muslim is obligated to carry out. It was the first time I felt I truly understood what they're trying to make us learn with student service learning. It's about helping the community around us.

But anyway, back to the biryani. We set the rice aside and added onions and chicken to two pots on the stovetop. It was actually less work than I expected. Once the chicken was tossed around a bit, we poured some water on, added the spices, and just let it simmer until it was ready to add the rice. Apparently, the community at the homeless shelter loved the spice blend we were using. And all the while, we chatted with each other and learned about one another, agreeing it's even nicer knowing somebody else will enjoy your cooking more than you will. Once the rice was added to the chicken mixture, we also added the same amount of water to cook the rice, and just let it simmer until the water was gone. I also made green beans during this time.

Once the biryani was done, everyone got a taste, and then it was packaged away into food trays for the homeless shelter. The biryani was a little milder than I was used to, but that was probably because at the shelter they didn't eat a lot of South Asian food, which tends to be spicy. It felt really good knowing that it would feed people who needed food the most. Making the biryani brought home to me that food can bring people together, but not only when you're eating it. Cooking it, chatting over a plate of it, and sharing it can be the most rewarding of all. I'll try and remember this the next time I'm eating my biriyani and waiting on my mother after Jummah!

Glossary:
Jummah: Congregational Friday Muslim prayer.
Masjid: Muslim place of worship.
Imam: Muslim faith leader.
Salaam-Alaikum/Walaikum-Salaam: Peace be upon you/And You.
Biriyani: South Asian savory rice dish.
Dahl: South Asian lentil dish.
Du'aa: Arabic word for prayer.
Zakat: One of the five pillars of Islam requiring Muslims to give a portion of their wealth to charity.

Where I'm From
Asha Smith
Herbert Hoover Middle School

I am from tea leaves,
From candles and colorful flowers.
I am from the frost on my windows every winter morning
From the mango trees in my home country,
And the dark pink rose bush outside our garage,
Whom I remember, never wilted alone.

I am from many diwali's and holi's,
From my mother and my father,
I'm from gift giving and planting seeds,
And from lots of laughter as a family.

I am from fantasies and tall tales,
And the voice of my grandmother, every night until I was four.
I'm from adventures,
I'm from India and Scotland.
I'm from idlis and dosas,
From Haggis and Cranachan,
And the sweet smell of a feast drifting through the house
from my mother's cooking.

I am from heirlooms,
From clothing and religion,
I am from ski trips and camping,
From amusement parks and ziplining.

The list of my memories are endless, for I have made many positive ones with the people I love.

I am me,
I come from a family of mixed cultures and traditions,
I love my family,
And I love myself.

Light In Me
Arya Das
Silver Creek Middle School

My light shines like a diya,
Filling me with joy and happiness
Wisdom that I share with others,
Eternally burning

It burns in me

My light is the gold on my saari,
That lines my faded blue blouse
With my hair worn long,
And my cherry red bindi,

It burns in me

My light is cooking,
Learning the recipes of my Ajji and Thakoma,
The highlighter shade of lemon rice,
With bright bitter and sour flavors,
The chicken tikka with pani puri,
The aloo gobi or palak paneer
Burning my tongue but popping with vivid spices

It burns in me

My light is Kuchipudi,
The songs of Lord Shiva,

Saraswati, and Ganesh,
Vishnu, Rama, and Krishna.
And my ankle bells chiming to the rhythm.
My feet beating to the drum,
As I watch the audience hearts be filled with joy.

It burns in me,

My light is madhubani,
With the intricate designs,
Like a maze of art
With running streams,
And calling birds
With the wide eyed style

It burns in me

My light is holi and diwali,
With the bright colors,
And millions of lights,
Were we pray and celebrate,
Connect with our loved ones.

This eternal light burns forever,
Showing truth and wisdom,
Having kindness and joy,
And shining with love.

A Proper Lady
Melanie Ouyang
Hallie Wells Middle School

"Sit straight," barked my mother, eyeing me up and down like a military sergeant. I silently glared at her and sat straighter, my eyes going from my phone to my mother.

"And," she began, "I saw your recent math quiz score." my heart tightened, and I gulped. I had not done so well on the recent math quiz, I got an eight out of ten which is unacceptable for my mother.

"I'll go retake it," I slowly said whilst looking at my mother's face, for even a hint of fury. It was quite obvious. She was furious.

"Lin Xiao Wei!" my mother yelled, it's been a long time since she last yelled my full Chinese name. Though, it's been a long time since I hadn't gotten full marks.

"I know, I know, I'll go retake, I promise mo-"

"Lin Xiao Wei, what is going on with you? An eighty percent on your math quiz? What are you doing? What is going on in that head?" she quickly walked over to me, her black high heels clacking against the wooden kitchen floor as she approached me. In a flash, she was in front of me and had already flicked her fingers against my forehead hard. My head was humming and I looked at her again, tears swirling in my eyes.

A tear rolled down my eyes and hit the hard wooden floor, "Fine! Go find your perfect little girl then!" I ran up the stairs and slammed the door behind me. I was huffing and puffing when I slammed myself against the bed and cried. My mother didn't come to get me, I didn't hear her, I couldn't see her, I didn't want to see her. I slowly rolled out of bed and walked over to the door, but instead of opening it, I locked it. I didn't want her to come in.

Suddenly, a trembling voice sounded outside, "Honey? Are you in there?" It was Grandma.

"Leave me alone!" I yelled back and ran to my bed.

"Honey…Please…Come talk with grandma…"

"No! Leave. Me. Alone!" I heard a sigh, and when I unlocked the door and checked outside, there was no one there. Instant regret hit me, and I knew I shouldn't have taken my anger out on Grandma. Since I could remember, Grandma has been there, taking care of me, comforting me, and helping me. My mother is a businesswoman, so she never had any time to take care of me. So she asked my grandmother to help her take care of me. This isn't abnormal, since most of the Chinese I know live with their grandparents, and it's fun to share with non-Chinese classmates at least.

I opened the door and walked out, to be met by my

mother. The person I wanted to see the least, was staring at me with lightning brewing in her eyes.

"Lin. Xiao. Wei." she was glaring at me, lasers shooting out of her glassy clear eyes. I right now have 2 options, 1 to apologize quickly and get it over with, or 2…

"What?" I responded, my eyes growing cold.

My mother stared at me furiously, "Who said you could talk to me like that?" I glared at her, "I did."

She laughed coldly as she stared at me, "You've got some nerve talking to me like that." "Learned from the best," I said.

"You're grounded."

"Alright fine," I shouted back and ran downstairs. When I got downstairs, I saw my grandmother cooking dinner. Since my mother is always so busy with her work, and I'm always so busy with schoolwork, classes, and others, my grandmother always takes care of all the chores. I stared at her hunched back, working away at the dumpling skins with great speed, a skill you develop when you've been doing it for decades.

She looked up at me and smiled, "Ah, Xiao Wei, you're here." I slowly walked over, "Grandma, I'm sorry…"

"Ah, it's okay, you were angry, I understand."

"I know...But I still shouldn't have screamed at you like that...It's disrespectful." "It's okay, I'm okay."

"How about I help you with the dumplings? As a representation of me being sorry," I smiled and said.

"Alright," she smiled back. We were making the dumplings from scratch, starting from the dough to rolling out the peels, making our stuffings, to boiling it. If you don't know, it's hard. Well hard for an ABC (American-born Chinese) like me. (Thank goodness grandma already made the dough for the dumplings, I have a talent for failing doughs for bread or anything basically)

"So we put the stuffing...here?" I asked.

"Oh no honey, that's too much, add a little less and add it here," she said lovingly, her wrinkles near her eyes folding, her hands gently leading mine, teaching me how to do it step by step.

"Mom's so evil! I hate her!" I complained to my grandmother as I gradually got the hang of making dumplings.

Grandma paused for a moment and looked at me with a complex expression, she slowly put down the dumpling peels, "Your mother can get angry sometimes but she still loves you. She teaches you manners."

"Grandma, are you seriously siding with her?"

"No, but you must understand- You know what…Nevermind…" "Let's just continue making dumplings grandma."

The following hours of making dumplings were in silence. I didn't want to talk to grandma, and she didn't say anything to me either. After we boiled the water, put the dumplings in, and ate dinner with mom, I did my homework and ran upstairs. At that moment, I thought that everyone in the house was against me, so I wanted to run away… So that was that, I swiftly packed my things, a notebook, a bag of food, a few bottles of water, a purse with a few hundred dollars in it, a laptop, a charger, a pack of pencils, an eraser, and a backpack that everything was stuffed into. I hid my backpack under my bed, and went to the bathroom to brush my teeth. My mother came into my room without knocking and sat on the small couch, in the corner of the room. My room isn't big, but it's enough to fit a desk, a bed, a small couch, and a chair that's pushed into the desk.

"Xiao Wei. I'm very disappointed in you today," my mother started. Here we go again, I rolled my eyes and continued to brush my teeth. Ignoring everything she was saying. I spit out the toothpaste, gurgled and rinsed. My mother sat there, legs crossed, staring at me as I walked out of the bathroom.

"Can you knock before you enter my room? Y'know, privacy?" I said dryly.

"This is my house, and so I go by my own rules. Do

you pay the bills? Do you spend your day working so you can provide for the family?"

"Stop guilt tripping me-"

"Lin Xiao Wei! Who taught you to speak to your elders like this? Remember what I've taught you since young-"

"Yeah, yeah. Respect your elders and blah blah blah. Now get out of my room! I'm about to take off my clothes to take a shower!" I screamed the last part. My mother stared at me, I could see hellfire burning in her eyes. I've grown up, I'm rebelling against her rules, her hardcore, stone like, Chinese ways. So she's angry. Really angry.

"Lin Xiao Wei. Don't think I won't hit you,"

"I'll call the police, I'll call the child abuse center then! I'll get you arrested! I'll tell them you abuse me, and you did many other crimes-"

"Enough! Lin Xiao Wei, you're grounded! Don't think about going out, don't think about going on your phone or computer! And don't think I don't know about those friends of yours. They are bad influence on you, and I forbid you from being friends with them,"

"What the heck mom?! Why? Just because I'm not your sweet obedient little girl anymore? I've grown up! Get over it!"

I pursed my lips and ran into the bathroom. This conversation was only fueling my anger and the thought of running away.

Before I came to the USA, I lived in China. In China, the competition to get into elite colleges was only by studying hard and getting the best score on the final exam in the third year of high school. Unlike in America, where I learned there are four years of high school, in China, we only had three years. The final year would determine whether we get into the best college or we end up going to some other school, which could be devastating for some families. The culture of education started, I don't know when but my mother brought it with her all the way from China, onto the plane to the country of freedom, our new home. America. Now, in China, you could always restudy a year to take the final exam again, but it would be the suffocating pressure on your shoulders all over again, and others would look down on you. My mother always told me that some of her classmates restudied and couldn't take the pressure, their scores didn't go up and instead went down. She always told me, "Don't be like them, they'll always be looked down upon in society. You don't want to be looked down upon."

My thoughts tore me back to reality, as I looked up and realized my mother had left already. I glanced at my backpack under my bed and took a shower. I closed my eyes as I laid on my bed, thinking about everything, my grades, my family, my life. I was drifting off into my dreams, where I had everything, my grades were perfect, and my mother was proud of me. I was happy. Suddenly I heard screaming. My dream started twisting and turning, I felt sick, it felt as if I was on a plane and it was about to crash land. I tried to open my eyes but I couldn't, I just felt a twisting, nausea feeling in my stomach. I almost threw up, when the twisting finally stopped, my head was hurting. It felt as if there was an earthquake in my head, my head felt as if I just had a fever. Or am I still going through it? I shook my head and sat up on my bed.

"Argh…My head hurts," I looked around the room, it was pitch black. I sighed and felt towards my bedside table, my hand felt around near the bed, searching for the clock so I could check what time it was. However, I couldn't find it. In fact, I couldn't even feel my bedside table! My heart skipped a beat, as when my eyes finally got used to the darkness, I found that this wasn't even my room. I couldn't process anything in my mind straight, but the next thing I knew, I was screaming. Very loudly. Like a freaking megaphone, you could practically hear my voice from China to the USA. A woman ran into my room. She didn't look too old, maybe 30 or 40 ish?

"Why are you screaming?" she asked, her face filled with confusion and irritation.

"Who are you! And why am I here?! DID YOU KIDNAP ME!" I continued to shout, ignoring the woman's questions. But, she suddenly came up to me and slapped me across the cheek. Leaving a reddish pinkish mark. I stared at the woman, mouth opened real wide.

"Shut up you wrench! I knew I should've left you for the streets…" The room was still dark, but I could recognize that face from anywhere. My mother.

"Mom, WTF!" I shouted back, "Just because I'm growing up-" another hard slap came across my face. This time I was stunned. The woman opened the curtains to the window, the dreary light of the morning barely came through.

"Listen here you wrench, just because you came outta me and call yourself my so-called daughter, does not mean you can eat, sleep, and drink for free in this household." she threw me a mop and demanded, "Now go clean the courtyard, and feed the chickens. And make your brother some breakfast while you're at it. He's going to the final exam of highschool today. My precious son is going to graduate with the highest marks!"

"What? Cook breakfast? In your dreams, why would I cook-" another slap landed across my face, and I squinted my eyes at the woman and started examining her more closely. She was a woman with short black curly hair and wrinkles around her face. She wore what looked to be farmer's clothing? What was going on?

"Now brat, go cook some breakfast."

"Whatever." and a few more slaps later I ended up in the kitchen…I looked around the kitchen, and of course, there was barely anything there.

A few days went by, and yeah I became their working slave. I swear this is against the law! But as I lived through these few days, I started noticing something...I was being called Lin Wen Lian, instead of Lin Xiao Wei. Lin Wen Lian, was...my mother's name...I couldn't find a single mirror around this place, maybe because they're broke or something, and their water...was unspeakably dirty. This place was like a hellhole, like I was in one of those labor camps in North Korea or something?! For a girl born in the 2030s, this is absolutely unacceptable! I decided that I needed to get to the bottom of this mayhem.

No, I didn't run away, and believe me I tried. I experienced just more beatings when I got caught. Apparently, this body is really frail and weak, these legs sure couldn't get me that far.

And yes, unfortunately I did figure out this: I'm my mom now? Well I guess reincarnated? Revived? Relived? I don't know what you want to call it, but I believed that I time traveled back to the past. My mother's past. And yes, I got beat a lot. But did that stop me? No way, as a 2033 independent asian female, I was determined to get back to my time. Yep, that was my goal the whole time. Now anyways, a few more weeks have passed and my mother's 'brother' finally went to take that final exam. You can't even imagine my mother's mother's face when her son went to take that exam. It was like he already took the test, got the best score and won the olympics alongside.

It was like: "Oh my son, make it back safe alright? Ah and make it there safe of course! Make mummy proud!

We'll have a ginormous feast waiting for you! We'll show your grades off to all the relatives.." and blah blah blah. You get the point don't ya?

Anyways, once he left, she turned towards me, or my mother in context, and glared at me coldly. She then handed me 10 dollars and told me to go buy groceries.

"Don't you dare steal anything from me you rat." she growled before leaving back inside the house. Like, what does she have? Rabies?

I went to the market and bought groceries, 4.95 dollars in total, or should I say yuan? And of course, I stole the rest of the money. What good person would ever buy groceries for that kid?

My mother's brother was a tall and skinny boy, he looked decent, with tanned skin, and shaggy hair but I could have a feeling that the way he looked at my mother, or myself at that moment, was a little weird. It made me have an uneasy feeling...Something bad was going to happen, and I just knew it, the way his eyes made me feel shivers down my spine, and jitters when I go to sleep. My mother and her brother weren't as simple as "siblings" or anything, my mother was the child of my mother's father and another woman's child. However, when they got caught, the woman gave birth to the child already, and ran away. My mother's brother however, was the child of her father and well her "mother", so technically, my mother isn't related to her mother.

Which I'm going to use to my advantage. So, when my mother's brother, or now my brother, came back from testing, I prepared a full on feast! Of course with a little twist of course. A few hours after those two ate, they felt sick and went to go throw up by the river or something. Last I heard from them was the mom cursing me out.

Something like: "AH! CURSE YOU LITTLE WRENCH! I WISH YOU WERE NEVER BORN! YOU ARE JUST LIKE YOUR MOTHER! A LITTLE WITCH!" But, who cares anyways? Anyways, the next few days were absolutely horrendous. I was surviving off of the few dollars I stripped from the 10. I then got kidnapped, sold, resold, almost killed, beat, kidnapped again, sold, resold, almost beat to death, and finally was saved by the police. By then, I was basically just a human body without a soul.

"Take her to the hospital immediately! Are you okay honey...?" the police asked desperately.

And with my last breath, or so I thought, I said the blessful, wonderful, magnificent, words of wisdom, that I will definitely graffiti on my house when I get back to my time, "Do I look okay?" and passed out.

When I woke up, I was in the police station, and I happily escaped, got caught, escaped, got caught, escaped, got caught, and escaped again! The police ran after me but I jumped into the river and got washed away. At this point of time, I just wanted to go home. I promised myself that when I go back to my time I was going to study hard, get into a good college, a good university, and live a happy life.

When I awoke, I was in another house. In front of me was a middle aged woman and a little girl. I'm not sure if I got kidnapped or I got adopted but I wasn't going to doubt it. I don't have a shelter right now, so I could use this to my advantage.

"Hi honey, I'm Miranda, and this is Miley." the middle aged woman said to me.

I looked at her with confusion, my hand on my head. I don't really remember whatever happened to me. I remember faintly being washed away into the river, and choking on the water. It was faint, still so I didn't mind it. For the next few months I lived with these 2. Miranda, divorced, single mother, and works different jobs to sustain a lifestyle. Her daughter Miley? A spoiled wannabe rich brat. I honestly question how she still has any friends with that attitude, but I guess a lot of people are poor around this place. All wanting to be friends with the rich, unknowingly befriending a cruel, 2 faced, wannabe asian barbie. After some time, I soon realized that still, in this family, I wasn't welcomed. Miranda, though on the surface seemed to be nice and comforting but all her actions clearly showed her spoiling her daughter. Sometimes, when there were only 2 drumsticks, she would give both to Miley. I would only get rice. Though, I was happy I got any food. Of course, all mothers would prefer their biological daughter more than an adopted one.

I would occasionally get bullied in the school

Miranda enrolled me in from here and there but I fought back. Thanks to my wonderful exercise every day, I eventually trained this frail body to be at least decent. It's still not as great as the body I had when I was still myself but whatever. You get what you get and you don't get upset. I really wonder how my mother was so frail back in the days but when she beats me up over me grades she's so ferocious. Anyways after a while I left. At this point, I was tired and helpless. I wanted to go home, to be free, to go back to my comfortable bed.

I wandered the streets for quite a while, and at this point I was basically out of money. I lived off scraps on the streets and fought over food with dogs and rats.

One day, I was nibbling off a piece of bread I stole from a bread shop when suddenly a voice sounded behind my poor homeless body, he said, "If you achieve the highest score on the final exam, then you'll get to go back to your time." and after that, he left. At that point I was too tired to do anything, the bread I stole wasn't barely enough, the owner was after me, and nobody was nice enough to spare me any food. At this point, I'd die before I start studying. I had to get a job, or some way of income. I begged everyone that passed by, though I got glares and gossip behind my back.

"Look at that girl, so disgusting."

"She probably got kicked out of her house." "No, maybe she just didn't study hard enough." "No, she was definitely just too lazy."

"Why are lazy girls like her still alive?"

"If I was her, I would just go die already. So embarrassing."

The sharp words got worse and worse, my mentality was on edge at this point. I could no longer keep up with my funny remarks I usually make, I could no longer smile like I used to, I could no longer confidently think of myself as a proud independent individual female from the 2030s. Right now I was a disgusting, poor, homeless, freak on the side of the road. And I was about to die if I didn't get any help. I had to go borrow from the gangs. I had to. It was my only chance of surviving. I borrowed $10,000 and fled to the school. At this time, the school fees weren't bad. Plus, my grades back in 203* weren't bad either. I was in highschool at the time. Plus, I spent most of my life in China. I can do this. I can get the highest score.

I studied hard, with the money I had left, which was a lot, I could survive. I studied whenever I could, when I was eating, when I'm using the restroom. I had no friends. I just needed to study, to go home, to get out of this hellhole. To see my mother. To apologize. For my rebellion, for everything. I must've hurt her so much. She experienced all this yet she was able to stand tall, and I'm not even sure I'll make it pass high school. The cultural revolution just ended, and China was in chaos. Mao Zhu Xi just died and all the children finally were put back in school. Though because everyone didn't study and were too busy making campaigns, everyone was behind. Except me, I remember. In the 2030s, I was still counted as a prodigy. I had a photographic memory, a wonderful memory. I was praised everywhere for it, and won multiple awards thanks to it.

I didn't like joining competitions in the past, but now I miss them more than ever. At least if I didn't get first place I wouldn't be threatened to never be able to go back to my old life. A year goes by and finally, I made it to the final exam. And also the day my debt is due. I owe too much now, I'm terrified. I don't want the gangsters to come and find me while I'm taking my test. The final exam is split into sections, those sections are split into days. There are a total of 3 days. But grades come after the teachers grade everything. I can only sit and pray, pray to god that I'll survive. If I have to hide, I will.

I entered the testing room, and it was filled with silence. Everyone was scared, some because they didn't study, others just simply because they're nervous. Me, I'm scared for my life. If I don't get the highest score, I'll most definitely die. Whether in an alleyway, or at my house.

If I don't die from starvation or something, I'm going to die from those gangsters. I didn't leave myself a second escape route, this is my only chance to live. I bet everything on this test.

Everything.

The test began, and everything was so smooth. Though the others, not so much. I heard groaning, and panicked whimpers. The clock was ticking, and so was my heart. Every tick the clock made, my heart tightened a bit. That day, my body was just moving about the hallways to the different testing locations, my hand was moving, my brain was spinning, my heart was racing. In total that day, my pencil broke at least 10 times. Luckily, I survived the first day. And the second day. And now the third day. During the test, big sweat beads were rolling down the side of my face.

The final question, I'm not sure on how to do it. I'm scared, if I fail, I might just die. I'm going to be stuck here, stuck in my mother's body, and be beaten to death in my mother's frail body. I chose to check over everything else instead, I was too scared of facing the question head on. The clock was ticking, now there was only 5 minutes left. I started to panic, I didn't leave enough time for me to finish the final question. The clock ticked, my pencil raced, the led scratching against the paper making heavy noises. Everyone turned to look at me, as the clock ticked, 5…4…3…2…1…STOP!

I lifted my pencil, the answer revealed under my sweaty, now led covered hand. I quickly turned the paper over, checked for my name and turned my paper in. I didn't look back. Now, I had to worry about surviving. I still had some money left over, but the debt date was around now.

I wasn't sure when, I wasn't paying much attention when they had said. That was a horrible idea. Now, I'm petrified. I planned to just wait it out. I asked a teacher that liked me a lot, whether I could stay at her house for a while. I lied and said that my mother was in the hospital and her house was near. I think she knew that I was lying, but let me anyway, this is the education culture in China. The teachers always like the students who have better grades.

I once saw this same teacher, hit another student on the hand with a ruler over and over again. I saw the student's hand blood red. I honestly don't know how the student's hand didn't bleed. But it left a scar. No one cared. Everyone had their own thing to do. They couldn't care less. The next few weeks, I waited it out. It was a slow process, but since I was living with the teacher, the day she notified me the grades were out, I ran to the school billboard to check. My heart was pounding against my chest as I ran up to the billboard. I looked up, at the top...

And there it was...First place...I looked to the right, class A, that's my class, testing room 8, that was also my room! But when I looked all the way to the section where it said name, it was not mine. Nor my mother's. It was Shao Xing Li. My heart shattered. At this moment, I didn't know what to do. I was going to die. My mentality broke, I looked down and saw my name in second place. My heart sank, as I looked at the points, just but one point. I lost. I'm screwed. I'm dead.

I dragged my heavy footsteps onto the streets, there were students all around me. Some I know from classes, others classmates I met in the hallway. I walked right past them and sat down at an ice cream shop.

"Hi sir, can I get 1 vanilla ice cream?" I asked politely.

"Of course, little girl! Ah, you must've just finished testing, am I correct? Did you get your score out yet? How did you do? Oh, I must be asking too much-"

I looked up at him and smiled, "I got second place in the exam. Second place."

"Oh that's wonderful!" he continued to say some more cheery things as he went to go make my ice cream, I wanted to break down.

I stared at my feet until my ice cream arrived, and paid. I took my ice cream and walked away gloomily. However, I felt more calm than I expected. Maybe I wasn't as scared of death as I imagined. I crossed the street to get to a cafe when suddenly I heard a lot of screaming. I felt a strong impact on my body and I went flying.

When I opened my eyes, I was floating. I was dead. I was free. I was...happy. I cheered excitedly, now I didn't have to be beaten to death by the debt collectors! I saw what happened, I was crossing the road but I got hit by a car. Whatever. It's a quicker death than getting beat to death I guess... I floated above my dead body, I floated above the car that hit me.

I saw police rolling in and I wanted to scream, "Don't arrest them! I'm happy they hit me! I'm free now!" But I couldn't. I was a ghost now.

The scene quickly started to fast forward, I got a job? What? But wasn't I dead? Didn't I die? Times were changing so quickly, in the work office, I was getting bullied. They didn't like me. My head was a mess, who am I? Why am I here? What is my purpose? What was my purpose? My head was ringing, the last thing I remember seeing was me getting fired. My heart sank at that moment.

I heard faint yelling, it got louder and louder, and louder, and louder, and louder. Until it was ringing in my ears. I slowly opened my eyes to see my mother staring at me, her eyes filled with tears. I was in a hospital room, my grandmother, mother, a bunch of nurses, and a doctor standing next to me.

"What happened?" I asked faintly.

My grandmother wiped her tears and explained how they found me with a high fever that wouldn't go down. And I was unconscious. Apparently, I had been lying in the hospital bed for 3 days. They thought I was never going to wake up.

Years later as I look back at this incident, I'm still not sure whether I was dreaming or if I actually traveled back in time. Even if it was real, I still cannot believe the culture shock I had, I can't believe how my mother even survived in those times. However, I did ask my mother and apologize for revolting against her. She said that the workplace I saw before I came back was when she came to america and gotten a job with Chinese to feel more comfortable. But, at the time other Chinese only saw each other as competition so did everything against each other.

"Eventually one of us got a manager position. But, she only bullied us worse. She wanted to bully us out of our jobs so she could be the best there. With no competition. She didn't see anyone else but us as competitors. So eventually I left, I don't know how the others are but I started a small business and now we're here! I met your father when I was trying to start my business up, he was the biggest investor. He believed in me, he trusted me, he was the best man I've ever met. We got married and had you, but he got very ill one day and passed...away." my mother looked very pained when she told the part involving my father. She must've loved him very much.

"So what happened after that?" I asked.

"Well, on his will he gave me two thirds of the stocks he had in my company so I'm the biggest investor," she took a breath.

"So what happened with the other third?"

"Well, he gave it to you," she smiled. I smiled back at her. Maybe this family isn't so bad after all.

"So that's why you should always respect your elders. The Chinese way."

8th Grade
Winners & Honorable Mentions

An American Accent
Hridaan Popuri
Thomas W. Pyle Middle School

I was in 3rd grade when I first heard what my accent actually sounded like. I still remember that day - it was my teacher's birthday, and the Room Parents had decided to create a video for her. All the kids had to send in a video of themselves reading a message about our teacher, and the parents strung it all together into one big video to show her.

When I say I heard what my accent actually sounded like, I don't mean that it was my first time hearing myself speak. I had heard myself speak many times before, but it was almost always just me speaking, so my accent didn't feel out of place. That wasn't the case this time, my distinct accent clearly out of place.

I went to an American School in Singapore, and almost all of the kids had an American accent. Watching the video, I listened intently, waiting for my video. I had always felt like I sounded the same as all the other kids, but that changed when my video finally came up.

"Happy Birthday! You're my favorite teacher ever …"

I focused on the sound of my voice. If all the American accents were water in the sea, my distinct Indian one felt like a large, disruptive wave. In half of the words, I emphasized the wrong parts. I couldn't pronounce the 'th' sound. When I said a word with the letter 's', it sounded like the letter 'z'. No one seemed to notice, but I did. I felt like a fish out of the water.

As the years passed in Singapore, my accent didn't seem to matter that much - there were a few Indian kids in my class every year, but they didn't have accents as thick as mine - even though I had only lived in India till I was 4, and that was probably because my parents had a very noticeable Indian accent. I remember that the summer of third grade was when it became my mission to fit in. I don't even understand today why I cared so much - in Elementary school, everyone was carefree, and no one really bothered about what others thought of them. My school was international, and as I got into fourth and fifth grade, the classrooms became a boiling pot of different accents - American, Australian, British, Chinese, and some Indian, though there were rarely more than four or five Indians in my class - most of them had been born in America anyways, so their accents were different than mine - it made me feel that even amongst Indians, my accent still stuck out like a sore thumb.

During the summer of fifth grade, my dad told me on the way back from piano practice that we would be moving to America after the end of seventh grade. I was looking forward to going back to the US but that changed at the start of sixth grade. My PE teacher wanted all of us to record a video where we introduced ourselves. I did, and then I listened to it to make sure I hadn't made any mistakes. I heard my Indian accent, and I remember that one of my friends asked me why I was blushing. They didn't seem to notice my accent - but I did, and that was when I wondered what the kids in America would think of it.

That was how, two days later, I found myself watching Home Alone, slurring my words in a rather pitiful attempt to have the accent of the thief with the weird tooth. Even though I failed that one time, it was only the start. Every weekend after that, I would watch an American movie and try to master that accent - whether it was the Southern accent from Forrest Gump or the Midwest accent from The Wizard of Oz, I would pause every five seconds and try to imitate what a character was saying.

By June of 2023, when my plane finally landed in Washington DC, I sounded nothing like I had two years ago. I had watched so many movies from all over the country that I wasn't even sure if I had a New England accent, or a Southern accent, or a Midwestern accent - it was like all those accents had fused together to create a new accent, one even I didn't recognize. But it didn't matter - I finally sounded American enough, or so I thought.

On my first day of school, I went to my homeroom, and sat next to another boy who looked exactly like me - brown-skinned with glasses. He said hi to me, and I noticed that he sounded slightly Indian. I asked him where he was born. Imagine my shock when he looked over and replied "San Francisco."

I couldn't believe that someone who had been born in California could sound so similar to how I had sounded all those years ago, but I pushed it out of my mind. In fourth period, I sat next to a blonde boy with an accent I couldn't place - all I could tell was that it was Scandinavian. I asked him where he was from, and he said that he was born in Indiana, but that he had lived in Europe for over half of his life.

In fifth period, most of the kids were Americans, yet they all had different accents - one boy had a very clear Southern accent, and another one had a California accent. In sixth period, there weren't that many American kids on the side that I sat on, and I heard a variety of different accents - from French to Indian to Italian. And, while I was worrying about accents, there were kids who were not even fluent in English, since it was not their first language. I wondered what turmoil must have gone on in their minds, to move to the US without knowing English. Were they as stressed out as I was about my accent? Probably more so because how would they make friends, how would they figure out what was happening in class, what the teacher was saying, and understand instructions? It suddenly struck me that when I looked at the larger picture, my obsession with speaking in the 'right' accent was just that, an obsession!

When I got home, I walked up to my bedroom, where I sat on my bed and began thinking. I had wanted an American accent for a long, long time. But after everything I'd seen today, I wasn't sure what an American accent even was - and I felt as thick as a brick.

I realized there was no universal American accent - just because one person might have a Southern accent and another had a New England accent, it didn't mean any of them were any less American. An Indian accent could be considered American. So could a Scandinavian accent. My accent before leaving Singapore would have been considered American here. If you considered yourself American, then your accent was already American.

And then, in my mind, I was back in my third-grade classroom, listening to my message for my teacher. I remembered how my video had been much longer than all the others - she had smiled for all the others, but when mine came up, and she heard what I had to say, she got all teary-eyed and I became the only kid she walked up to to hug and thank. That was when I figured out that she hadn't noticed my accent at all - all she had noticed was that the message had come from my heart, and that was all that mattered.

And I realized that all my efforts of the past two years had been pointless. I had spent so long trying to create an American accent - and I hadn't realized that in this country, a melting pot of different accents, I had already had one.

Different
Lila Briskin-Watson
Silver Creek Middle School

Almost one hundred years ago,
Masses of people
Woven together by shared beliefs, filled trains
Fearing what would come next
Hoping for something resembling the villages where they'd lived
What they arrived to was
Different.

On Saturday, I go to synagogue.
When I arrived, I saw something I'd never noticed before
A police car giving me a cold hard stare.
It makes me see this place
Different.

When my friends come for Chanukkah, they cut latkes into small pieces
And make weird faces at the food, like exploring uncharted territory
"Ewww!" They chuckle.
"You don't like it?" I ask.
"It's not bad," They pause.
"It's just
Different."

In a land very far away Israelis and Palestinians are killed.
Little cubs and big lions gone too soon
At home, students are afraid to wear the Star of David.
Where I live, over and over, kids scrawl swastikas across
desks and walls. I hoped things would be
Different.

It's been almost one hundred years
Since everything was taken from my ancestors
Including their lives.
But today, I look around,
And I wonder, are things
Different?

Paper Crane Wishes
Jenny Ryu
Herbert Hoover Middle School

It's been exactly one year, seven months, and seven days since we flew away from everything. Leaving was the thing that tore my whole life down the middle, ripping it into the Before and the After. Ma says our new "home" is here, but that's not true. Home is where wet markets and smelly fish crowd the streets. Home is where the monsoon season brings warm, golden, rain. Home means my language. My school. My Before. Home is not here.

I feel this very strongly as I walk down Deer Road at night. It's nothing like Singapore. For one, it is empty. Even at the oddest hours of night, the city was full to the brim and bursting over in color. Here it is quiet. Colorless. Sad fluorescent lights rise like lanterns in the mist, hunching over the road. There is no one else for as far as I can see. I suddenly feel alone, like I'm the last girl alive in the whole world, and I want to turn back. But I'm here on a mission, so I grit my teeth and keep going. Four lefts and a right bring me to The Bridge.

It's only been a little more than a year, but I feel as if my whole ten years in Singapore was a dream. When I sleep, my dreams are here, in quiet, lonely, Washington State. When I talk, the words once set into my bones start to slip through my grip.. But I remember, and I'll never forget, the stories. Words have always been what came naturally to me.

Back in my old school, I used to tell tales of magical creatures and wise trees to the little kids. But my favorite stories were about the Wishing Game. To grant a wish, you must give up something of equal value in exchange. And I have never, ever, in my whole ten (and a half) years of life needed magical assistance more than now.

Exchanges must take place in special places where magic is ripe. That's why at twelve twenty-eight in the morning, I'm at the most magical place in the whole of my neighborhood, The Bridge. The Bridge is the place where on the Fourth of July, five months ago, the sky lit up like the stars had fallen to the ground. The place where I sit by myself on days where I miss home, and the trees below whisper, almost like humans, reminding me that I'm not alone. There's something magical here, I can tell.

The air is hard and frosty up on the edge. I sigh, and my breath fogs like a dragon's, hovering for a moment like a cloud over the shadowy trees below. It's a dark night, and when my fingers start to throb from the cold, I wonder if this was a bad idea. My mind whirls and tumbles ahead, pushing only the bad, scary thoughts to the top. The trees circling my bridge begin to look like knobbly old hands, clawing their way through the earth. The night is too dark, so dark it feels heavy. I can't shake the feeling it was a bad, bad idea. A bad idea to come to this bridge, a bad idea to come to this country. The air around me freezes when I feel something behind me.

I felt the magic first. I can't describe it in words that will make sense. It's the feeling of free falling through the air, hurtling faster, faster. Like my heart became a Chinese firecracker, lit up and booming. Like I was weightless.

My lungs burn from holding my breath, but I don't look back. I can't. I don't dare. The dead, crisp leaves call to me. The dark, stormy river calls to me. What is your wish? What is your wish?

"I..." I start. My mind whirls through a thousand different options. There's a million things I could wish for. Speaking English better. Fitting in at school. Lunchables instead of rice. Being fully American. Being fully Singaporean.

But I don't say any of these things. Instead I scrunch my eyes tight, and blurt, "I wish for a friend."

I never thought friends would be a problem for me. But because I can't really speak English, I've spent lunch alone in the library, flipping through books I can barely read. Been last to the pick in P.E. Last to pick in general, really.

I pluck out my offering. It's a paper crane my auntie gave me back home. I cradle the delicate red paper between my fingers. It feels like a part of myself, and I really don't want to give it away. But maybe that's what I need to do, to really belong here. I drop the crane and watch the cold, tumbling river carry it off. It feels like I just trashed the most beautiful diamond necklace in the world, instead of cheap red paper. My eyes prick with tears that sting in the cold.

It didn't work. Nothing changed. No magical golden light or flying origami fish. No friend either. My brain throbs, and I'm tired. Maybe the stories were just stories, like Ma says. I grab my bag to go back to my house.

"Hey!" A voice shouts from the other side of the bridge. "Hey! Cai! You dropped this!"

It's Christopher, one of the kids from school. In his hands he's holding the red paper crane, soggy, but still whole. My whole body gasps in a breath that I didn't know I was holding.

I want to say so many things. Thank you. What are you doing here? Why are you talking to me? But instead I mutter an "...Oh."

He gives me a sheepish grin, and says, "I was just walking there-" he makes a vague gesture towards the bottom of the bridge, "My house is there, I wasn't, like, stalking you or something. I saw your origami. It's pretty good actually. I was wondering um- do you want to make some at lunch tomorrow?"

"...Ok. Yeah, I would like that." I say with a smile. It's not perfect, I still have my accent, but I don't care. Maybe I don't have to be all the way American or Vietnamese. Maybe I can be both.

I take the crane with both hands and cradle it between my fingers again. I smile and Christiphore smiles too. Maybe my wish did come true.

The "Lagom" Culture
Lucie Vidh
Cabin John Middle School

Everyone strives for balance in their lives assuming that it will make life better. Sweden, in this case, is not an exception. "Lagom", in Swedish, translates to "balance" or "in moderation." It is not only a common term, but a lifestyle. It is a word that illustrates the many intricacies of Swedish life (which we will get back to later). Although this lifestyle makes up most of Swedish culture, it can be a hit or miss for foreigners. This comes to a surprise to many, as again is balance not what we seek for everyday?

The "lagom" culture aims to balance every juncture and area of daily life. It is based on moderation, sustainability, and social awareness. There cannot be too much or little of something; it must be "lagom" or "just right." It seems wholesome in the beginning but what foreigners eventually come to understand is that it is taken extremely seriously in Sweden and Swedes try to marry this philosophy with essentially everything. This can relate to anything as trivial as the amount of butter on their knäckebröd in the morning to something as paramount as their emotions. Though it might sound extreme, it is what I (and most Swedes) grew up with. It is the environment that I feel most comfortable in. However, despite the whole point of the lifestyle is to minimize stress, following it came with its own major ups and downs.

I've found that the "lagom" lifestyle taught me many of my core morals. It taught me to be independent, to value traditions, to live in the moment, to not be driven by a materialistic mindset, and to be highly altruistic. I remember vividly when I was little in our small neighborhood in the outskirts of Stockholm. Our house sat on top of a big hill with our road snaking down with houses on each side. The trees became increasingly bare as leaves of red, brown, and yellow piled up. Hot summer air began turning into chilly winds, reminding us that summer was ending and allowing us time to prepare for the next few tough winter months. By this time of year it was mid-Fall, as well as the time for our annual neighborhood leaf clean up. Every year, my family and our neighbors would rake all of the dead leaves and help with each other's lawns together. Though difficult work, it was incredibly gratifying to not only have an organized neighborhood but also to get to know each other in the process. This was only one of many humble yet prominent traditions that shaped my life and character in Sweden.

However, as I mentioned earlier, it was not all sunshine and rainbows. The "lagom" culture also caused a huge rift among myself and others as there were some norms that I couldn't seem to quite nail. An example of this was that you could never outshine anybody else as again, there cannot be too much or little of something. Now, you may be thinking: "Isn't this normal in most cultures?" Well, while this is certainly true, I think that we can both agree by now that Sweden does not do anything haphazardly. Swedes would go far enough as to not recognize the accomplishments of others because it was viewed as gloating. A Swedish family friend of ours who was incredibly skilled in swimming and had won several Olympic medals refused to ever speak of her accomplishments in fear of being looked down upon for "bragging." She's only one example out of many who struggled with this cultural custom. I observed the same thing happening with my friends, teachers, family members, and even strangers. I even found myself doubting my own achievements due to said custom. It was an extremely damaging mindset and still haunts many in Sweden today, as well as myself at times.

Historically, Sweden was a very homogenous country. There was a large lack of diversity, and it has only started appearing more in the last 50 years or so. Nevertheless, this led to a society where deviating from the norm was highly criticized and a lot of this was largely fueled by the "lagom" culture. Despite the deep influence that my Swedish culture has had on me, my mothers French heritage has certainly left a mark of its own. Ironically, my French Caribbean inheritance entirely juxtaposes my Scandinavian roots (which has always made me question how my parents even got along in the first place but that is a story for another time). This is due to the fact that compared to my Swedish family, my French family is incredibly rambunctious and passionate. Despite this, they've taught me manners, how to speak up for myself, and that family is everything. Fortunately, I was able to find a healthy balance between both my Swedish and French Caribbean roots through the help of my family and diverse friend group. However, the same cannot exactly be said for my mother, who was immediately deemed an "outsider" once she moved to Sweden.

As a European woman with blonde hair and blue eyes, my mother would've never imagined the culture clash to be so extreme. My mother is very vocal, direct, extroverted, highly forward-thinking, and sparks small talk any chance she gets. This was not taken so kindly by the Swedes as this was not emphasized in the "lagom" lifestyle. Unlike the French culture that my mother was so used to, Sweden is a very egalitarian society. While she expected men to hold the door open for her it only resulted in her dismay when they were shut in her face. To most cultures, this might be incredibly shocking, but to Swedes it is only meant to reinforce equality between genders. Unfortunately, my mother has too many stories to share about her experiences while living in Sweden that I can write in a straight-forward and comprehensive essay. However, her story mirrors the experiences of many other foreigners who found themselves lost in the "lagom" culture, lacking further information on it before being plunged head first into the rushing tide.

Now that I live in America with the French part of my family, I've generally lost touch with the "lagom" culture. I definitely miss it because it essentially made up my childhood but looking back at it, I'm happy that I've mostly let it go. I would not be able to live happily and successfully if I tried integrating it now as much as I did in the past. However, do not mistake the "lagom" culture as a culture of dogmatism. The examples I included were of both extremes as they were what stood out to me while I lived in Sweden. The lifestyle is changing as the years go by and Swedes are generally not so extremist in current times. If you find yourself struggling with the daily stresses of our modern world, try out the "lagom" lifestyle. I hope this essay gave you more insight into my childhood, my culture, and possibly introduced you to a new way of living

Untitled

Luna Hernandez

Forest Oak Middle School

"I love your culture"
But you pick and choose
You wear our jewelry ignorantly
don't bother to learn its significance
You say "Spanish is so sexy"
But make fun of my mother's broken English
You love to eat our food and post it on your socials
#cultured!
But what about when you made fun of how it smelled
when I took it to school for lunch
You say you want a "spicy Latina" But stereotype Hispanic women as
Fiery, loud, and vain
You say our dancing is beautiful
But then turn around and call it promiscuous
My people are suffering in Cuba, Venezuela, Honduras
And you do nothing.
Why?
"They'll steal our jobs"
You love my culture
But only when it's convenient for you.

With Closed Eyes I Remember
Sophie Levine
Thomas W. Pyle Middle School

A shiver runs down my backbone,
separating at my legs and whisking away
down towards my feet,
tingling in my arms,
as the last drops of sunlight slowly
fade
beneath
the horizon.

Pinpricks of light appear in the
vast, dark, sky
I can see them through the window,
from the worn
wooden
dining room table, the

first

three

stars.

My brother yells for our parents
to come in,
"It's time," he says, bursting with excitement.

Shabbat is nearly over.
The week is coming to a close,
but the ceremony of Havdalah
is about to begin.

My hands find our special Havdalah candle:
braided of 6 strands-
varying shades
of blue and white
six wicks-
all coming together.

It's waxy body
tingles
with memories from within.

The time we were out
of grape juice,
and Mom got out some carrot juice:
the thick orange liquid so
strange looking that
no one dared drink it
but her.

And the
very first
time Micah held
the bursting bright flame
on his own
and my heart swelled with pride
to see him do it,
and my mouth hurt from the

size of my grin.

It's time.

The lights are off.
We see only by the
shining flame of our candle,
it's brilliant light illuminating the table
casting a
soft golden glow
over everything.

As we chant the blessings
the rich melodious notes swirl through the air
wafting up to the ceiling and
drifting down around us,
offering comfort-
like a good book read
too many times
to count.

The sweet words blossom around us,
bringing us together,
tasting of home.

Maybe our ancestors sang these words,
through joyful occasions
and more painful ones.
Maybe we can too.

Their melody a string
that connects us,

connects us,
to who we are

We lean in closer,
arms over each other's shoulders ,
we feel the light spread
throughout our bodies-
and know the flame is no longer on the candle,
but in us,
spreading its warmth
from head to toe,
bringing us unity.

Tonight we find the resolve to keep going,
to have happiness
in the week ahead.

The scars we hold,
the weight that burdens us
melts away
as we sing the sacred blessings.

As we chant the touching melody,
we carry the light of the Sabbath with us,
keep it close.

And as we sing the last words
I lift the candle and dip the flame
into our cup of grape juice:
the tiny hissing,
sputtering sound it releases
the last sounds of our old week,

as it finally melts into the new.

Shabbat is over.

But the fragrance of our spices
hangs in the air
long after the candle is out.

The sweet words of
Eliyahu Hanavi
fill the air as we rejoice.
Shabbat is over,
but a new week has come
and whatever happens,
we will see it through.

Whatever happens,
we will be strong enough.

Strong enough,

Together.

INDEX

Cabin John Middle School
Lucie Vidh, Essay** — 115

Eastern Middle School
Kristian Carpenter, Essay** — 38
Lawrence Liao, Poem+ — 11
Florence Ou, Short Story* — 20
Sofia Ou, Short Story* — 66
Juno Seigel, Essay* — 58

Forest Oak Middle School
Luna Hernandez, Poem** — 120

Frances Scott Key Middle School
Aria Roy, Poem** — 47

Hallie Wells Middle School
Reya Ganesh, Essay** — 41
Melanie Ouyang, Short Story** — 81
Dilshan Prakash, Short Story** — 50

Herbert Hoover Middle School
Khanh Pham, Essay** — 31
Jenny Ryu, Short Story* — 111
Asha Smith, Poem** — 77

Julius West Middle School
Mithran Karthic, Essay* — 14
Ella Zimmerman, Essay** — 34

Silver Creek Middle School
Jitu Abebe, Poem* — 61
Lila Briskin-Watson, Poem* — 109
Arya Das, Poem** — 79

Thomas W. Pyle Middle School
Madeleine Lee, Poem** 45
Sophie Levine, Poem** 121
Hridaan Popuri, Essay* 104
Westland Middle School
Sufyana Johnson, Essay** 74

* Winner
** Honorable Mention
+ Best in Show

Made in the USA
Middletown, DE
05 August 2024

58570443R00076